THE

WITCH'S
ALTAR

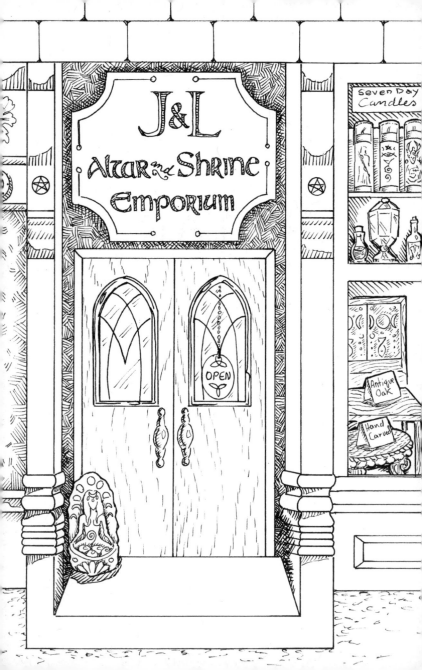

© Tymn Urban

JASON MANKEY has been a Pagan and a Witch for over twenty years and has spent much of that time writing, talking, and ritualizing across North America. He's a frequent visitor to a plethora of Pagan festivals, where he can often be found talking about Pagan deities, rock and roll, and various aspects of Pagan history. He is currently the editor of the Patheos Pagan channel and can be found online at his blog, *Raise the Horns*.

© Carrie Meyer/Insomniac Studios

L AURA TEMPEST ZAKROFF is a professional artist, author, dancer, designer, and Modern Traditional Witch. She holds a BFA from the Rhode Island School of Design, and her myth-inspired artwork has received awards and honors worldwide. Laura blogs for Patheos as *A Modern Traditional Witch* and Witches & Pagans as *Fine Art Witchery* and contributes to *The Witches' Almanac*. She is the author of the bestselling book *Sigil Witchery: A Witch's Guide to Crafting Magick Symbols* as well as *The Witch's Cauldron: The Craft, Lore & Magick of Ritual Vessels*. *The Witch's Altar* is her third book, and her fourth, *Weave the Liminal: Living Modern Traditional Witchcraft*, will be released in early 2019. Find out more at www.lauratempestzakroff.com.

WITCH'S
ALTAR

The Craft, Lore & Magick
of Sacred Space

JASON MANKEY
LAURA TEMPEST ZAKROFF

Llewellyn Publications
Woodbury, Minnesota

FIRST EDITION
First Printing, 2018

Cover design by Shira Atakpu
Cover illustration by Mickie Mueller
Interior illustrations by Mickie Mueller and Llewellyn Art Department

Llewellyn Publishing is a registered trademark of
Llewellyn Worldwide Ltd.

Library of Congress Cataloging-in-Publication Data

Names: Mankey, Jason, author. | Zakroff, Laura Tempest, author.

Title: The witch's altar : the craft, lore & magick of sacred space / by Jason Mankey and Laura Tempest Zakroff.

Description: First edition. | Woodbury, Minnesota : Llewellyn Worldwide, [2018] | Series: The witch's tools series ; # 7 | Includes bibliographical references.

Identifiers: LCCN 2018027545 (print) | LCCN 2018035816 (ebook) | ISBN 9780738758336 () | ISBN 9780738757964 (alk. paper)

Subjects: LCSH: Witchcraft. | Altars.

Classification: LCC BF1566 (ebook) | LCC BF1566 .M2764 2018 (print) | DDC 133.4/3—dc23

LC record available at https://lccn.loc.gov/2018027545

Llewellyn Worldwide Ltd. does not participate in, endorse, or have any authority or responsibility concerning private business transactions between our authors and the public.

All mail addressed to the author is forwarded, but the publisher cannot, unless specifically instructed by the author, give out an address or phone number.

Any internet references contained in this work are current at publication time, but the publisher cannot guarantee that a specific location will continue to be maintained. Please refer to the publisher's website for links to authors' websites and other sources.

Llewellyn Publications
A Division of Llewellyn Worldwide Ltd.
2143 Wooddale Drive
Woodbury, MN 55125-2989
www.llewellyn.com
Printed in the United States of America

Other Works by Jason Mankey

Transformative Witchcraft: The Greater Mysteries
(January 2019)

The Witch's Book of Shadows (2017)

The Witch's Athame (2016)

Other Works by Laura Tempest Zakroff

Books

Weave the Liminal: Living Modern Traditional Witchcraft
(January 2019)

Llewellyn's 2019 Witches' Spell-a-Day Almanac (artist)

Sigil Witchery (2018)

The Witch's Cauldron (2017)

The Witches' Almanac (contributing author, 2017–2020)

Coloring Books

Myth & Magick (2016)

The Art of Bellydance (2016)

Witch's Brew (2016)

Steampunk Menagerie (2015)

Instructional DVDs

DecoDance (2015)

Bellydance Artistry (2011)

JASON MANKEY: *To all of my roommates over the years and whoever gave me the altar. Also special thanks to the many cats who have been a part of my life—Scarlet, Princess, Evie, and Summer—all of whom climbed on at least an altar or two.*

LAURA TEMPEST ZAKROFF: *For all of the new Witches out there figuring out how to do the thing—may you find your own way with both confidence and grace. Also to my beloved cat Sam, who managed to smash a statue of Lilith and lived to meow about it. Sacred things go on altars, and clearly that includes him.*

CONTENTS

INTRODUCTION

Two Witches, One Book
(Tempest)

Most books that are written by two authors in the Witch/ Pagan world tend to be by people who are partnered, or by people who work together in the same tradition, coven, or similar group. Well, that's not us, in either case. Jason is a Gardnerian Witch and I'm a Modern Traditional Witch, so we usually come at things from very different backgrounds. But we have found that besides both of us having long, curly locks, we often share common ground in vision, practicality, magick, and sarcasm.

Writing a book together started off as a bit of a joke around the time Jason was working on his second book in this series

(*The Witch's Book of Shadows*, his first being *The Witch's Athame*) and me on my first (*The Witch's Cauldron*). We were each writing contributions for the other's book, and started trading thoughts about the series in general. In sharing our most and least favorite parts to work on, we realized maybe we could collaborate on a book! We carried the laugh over to our beloved editor, who probably rolled her eyes at the email (with love) and then told us to finish the books we were working on.

We eventually ~~wore down the resolve of~~ won over our editor with the idea for this book. (I'm not saying it was cat photos that did it, but it may have been cat photos.) I believe it's fair to note that this book may have been inspired by whiskey, shared ritual, and late late nights with Pwords.

We both geek out hugely about altars and share an addiction to statues. The ideas for this book just flowed out of us. The fact that we come from different paths and backgrounds only helps strengthen the breadth of material presented here for you, the reader. Whether you work in a group or by yourself, practice ceremonial magic or fly by the seat of your cauldron, there's advice in here just for you. We think it's especially helpful to recognize that there isn't just one way to use, view, or build an altar. When we present different perspectives, it's not meant to confuse you, but to illustrate that there are many options and ideas at your disposal. That sense of awareness and freedom truly is the spirit you want to tap into when crafting and working your own Witch's altar.

The Old Trusty Altar (Jason)

My wife, Ari, and I have seven altars in our house. Some are dedicated strictly to magickal operations and others are representative of the changing seasons and the deities we personally honor. One of those seven altars is in my office, and is stocked mostly with magickal items that are meant to spark creativity and keep me writing. (The fact that this book is in your hands means they've probably done their job.) But one of our altars means more to us than the others, and it's such an important part of our practice that we refer to it as *the* altar.

The altar is a rather banged-up rectangular table that is two feet high and measures thirty-two by twenty inches. It's surprisingly solid for such a small table, and we've had people sit on it during ritual without any problem. I have no idea what type of wood it's made of, but that wood is rather pale and sometimes hard to see under the paint splatters. Yeah, *the* altar has a lot of white specks of paint scattered all over it, not to mention multiple dings, nicks, and scratches. (Thank the gods for altar cloths.)

The weirdest thing about this particular altar is that I have no idea where it came from. During my college years and for

3
. . .

Altar, before and after

about ten years after that, I generally lived in large, old houses with several roommates. In one of those houses our altar showed up one day, lost to the passage of time as an ordinary end table. For several years it did very little but collect magazines and serve as a home for the lamp parked next to the couch.

One of those houses hosted dozens of Witch rituals over the years, almost always in our living room, where the end table sat. Originally we used the table as an altar because it was convenient. It was *right there* in the room we were doing ritual in, so why would we use anything else? Once the ritual ended, the magazines and lamp went right back on the table, but somewhere along the way I realized that I really liked using this little table as an altar. It was just about the right size, and was tall enough that I didn't have to bend over every time I had to pick something up.

A few years after we started using our end table in ritual, we moved into a new house, one with a more dedicated working space. Our table still pulled double duty, but we liked it so much that we'd move it from the living room into our ritual room on sabbats and esbats. When we moved to California three years later, the altar table was one of the few pieces of furniture to go with us.

A year after moving to California, my wife and I established a new coven, with its rites and rituals eventually moving into the guest bedroom of our house. When we set up that room, our end table completely transformed into an altar. There was no question what was going in the center of the room and what our coven's altar was going to be. Several months later, while setting up our working space one night, I remarked to my coven-brother Matt that Ari had sometimes contemplated getting rid of our coven's primary working altar. His reply was, "Oh no, it's never going anywhere."

He wasn't quite right about our altar never going anywhere. I love it so much that I take it to other places. Every day our altar holds our primary working tools (like athames, books of shadows, and cauldrons), absorbing their energies. Our rituals literally revolve around our altar, and the magick we've stirred up over the years has contributed to its power. It's fair to say that our altar has a definite presence now, even when its less distinguished features aren't being covered up by an altar cloth.

With only a couple exceptions, our altar has been at every ritual our coven has celebrated, and it's the only tool we have that has been a part of every rite in our house. I have three athames, and Ari and I have nine chalices between us, but we have only one working altar. When Tempest and I discussed writing a book together, I took one look at my old, beat-up altar and knew what we would be writing about. Altars are often undervalued and overlooked, but they are one of a Witch's most powerful tools.

My altar most likely came from one of my friends, and coincidently, when Tempest and I were putting together this book, we knew we'd need the help of our friends to write it. To that end, this volume includes many alternative looks at altars under the heading "Altar-natives," all written by witchy friends of ours. I think they add a lot to the book and really help set the table when it comes to providing a thorough understanding of the altar and just what it can do for us as Witches.

CHAPTER ONE

What Is an Altar?
(Tempest)

aking altars and other kinds of sacred space often comes very naturally to Witches. Ordinary pieces of furniture get transformed into something extraordinary. On our journeys we gather together pieces of nature: crystals, stones, shells, bones, twigs, and leaves. We assemble them around statues of gods and collect them in jars and bowls, creating elaborate arrangements. Candles and incense, oils and resins, ignite the space. Photos of loved ones, inspiring pictures, and treasured finds and trinkets all find a home. Tools such as wands, athames, and cauldrons lay in waiting, nestled alongside tarot cards, pendulums, and other systems of divination.

We tend to transform our homes and workspaces into metaphysical masterpieces. What might start on one shelf in a bedroom frequently spreads to the window in the bathroom, a niche in the kitchen, an area on the porch, and the dashboard of the car—little altars everywhere. But how often do we actually stop and think about what an altar actually is?

Merriam-Webster defines an altar as "a usually raised structure or place on which sacrifices are offered or incense is burned in worship," as well as "a table…which serves as a center of worship or ritual." Essentially, an altar is a specified structure that a sacred activity takes place on or is focused around. According to that definition, places where you are mainly collecting items and assembling them may not technically be considered altars if they're not also specific structures where acts of worship or ritual take place, though people have a lot of different ideas about what worship and ritual are and what qualifies as sacred.

For example, consider the following words that are often used to describe sacred space:

Shrine: A shrine is considered to be a place that is made sacred by its associations with a deity, holy person, or relic. It can be a box, case, receptacle, corner, room, or building. A shrine is often designated as a place of devotion to a specific saint or deity, and may house a relic pertaining to that spirit. For example, the bones of a saint, a piece of a saint's blessed clothing, and similar items are all considered to be relics. Or the shrine may be a place where that person or spiritual personality was born, died, or appeared. Because of this association, people may make a pilgrimage to the shrine as part of their devotional practice.

Sanctuary: A sanctuary is a consecrated place, usually the most sacred place in a temple or church. It can also be a place where worship services are held. In addition, it has the connotation of being a safe place, offering protection, reset, and preservation.

Tabernacle: A tabernacle can be defined as a temporary dwelling place or receptacle for a deity. The word comes from the Latin *tabernaculum*, meaning "hut" or "tent," with the sense of it being a tent in which to gather for sacred purposes. In the book of Exodus in the Hebrew Bible, the Tabernacle is referred to by the word *mishkan*, meaning "residence," "dwell," or "rest." The Tabernacle was used during the Jewish people's journey through the wilderness until the building of Solomon's Temple in Jerusalem. Not only was it a temporary kind of temple, but it also housed the Ark of the Covenant. In Catholic churches as well as churches of some other denominations of Christianity, the place where the Eucharist is stored is also called a tabernacle. Because of this association, I like to call tabernacles the "bread box of God," much to my mother's consternation.

Temple: A temple is a building devoted to the worship of a god or multiple deities. It can also be considered a dwelling place for the divine, a place of education, and a repository for spiritual knowledge.

Reliquary: A reliquary is, most simply, a container for relics, usually designed with portability in mind—particularly for processions on special days and for ease of displaying relics to the public.

Ofrenda: Spanish for "offering," an ofrenda is a ritual altar where items are placed in honor of the dead and offerings are made during the celebration of Dia de los Muertos.

Stupa: From the Sanskrit word for "heap," a stupa is a Buddhist place of meditation that is a mound-like earthen structure. Stupas typically contain relics of Buddhist monks or nuns.

Grotto: From the Italian *grotta*, a grotto is a small picturesque cave, usually dedicated to a deity or saint. It can be an artificially constructed structure located in a park or garden, or an indoor structure that is made to resemble a natural cave.

Grove: A sacred grove is a grouping of trees that are believed to have special religious importance. Groves are found throughout the world. They can be naturally occurring or designed as a landscape feature. In several traditions

Grove and circle

a practicing group may be called a grove—referring to the interconnectivity of the trees in an actual grove and their rooted formation.

Circle: A sacred circle or sphere is a space ritually marked out by practitioners. The circle is believed to be able to contain energy, protect those working within it, and separate those activities from mundane happenings. A circle can be temporary and invisible, or made permanent and visible by building physical structures to define the space. Similar to a grove, it can also be used to describe a group of people working together.

There are so many different words to describe sacred places and practices! It says a lot about most societies and cultures that we habitually want to create a distinction between the sacred and the secular. We constantly seem to be seeking to define and determine what is sacred—but how distant the sacred is from our daily lives depends so much on our beliefs. If we see the world as mainly profane or unclean, and separate from the divine, then that creates a very specific mindset about how we see the divine and ourselves. Entering sacred space becomes somewhat of an ordeal, with many layers of separation between us and the divine. But if we find the divine all around us, then sacred space becomes more accessible, though not less special. For Witches and Pagans, the altar is a way for us to focus our attention and our practices, versus designating sacred/profane space. We see these sacred places as ways to connect more deeply to the divine without distraction, and to recognize more profoundly the presence of the divine in our lives.

Which leads us to this question: *Who gets to define how we connect or commune with the divine aspects of our world?* The short answer is you do. What exactly constitutes worship or ritual to you will determine what is or isn't an altar or a shrine. It shouldn't matter if you see yourself as a priest/priestess or not, or if you hold X number of degrees or are just starting to figure things out. We know that religious practices vary widely from culture to culture and can look and feel very different depending on a person's station, practice, and rank. It's important not to automatically designate one type of practice or protocol as the only one.

To give you an example of this, I'm going to share with you some of my own religious background and early experiences. I grew up in the Catholic Church and, until I was eighteen, attended mass regularly with my mother (or else). Catholic churches are well known for their often elaborate designs, with a huge visual focus on the main altar, which is typically elevated for all to see, generally with a statue, symbol, or painting of Jesus directly behind it. Use of the altar is restricted to the priests, acolytes, and Eucharistic ministers. The same is true for the tabernacle. Off to the sides there are special nooks—shrines that are usually dedicated to the Virgin Mary and whatever saint the church may be named in honor of. (Sometimes they throw Joseph—Jesus's stepdad—a bone and give him a place too.) My grandmother's church also had a host of saint statues in the back wings, because the more the merrier. These special places for Mary and the other saints are meant to be more accessible to the community, and are not restricted to only the clergy. Typically, offerings (which can qualify as sacrifices) and prayers can be made by anyone willing to visit with them.

But the big focus for everything is that big altar—where the main event takes place. Accounting for illness, high holy days, weddings, and funerals, I have witnessed the rite of transubstantiation at least a thousand times. Transubstantiation is the moment in the Catholic mass when the wine and the Eucharist (communion wafers) are said to be transformed (altered!) into the actual body and blood of Jesus Christ through the actions of the priest. Then everyone who has gone through the sacrament of Holy Communion can queue up to ingest these items, a few steps down and away from the altar. (If you look at the whole thing from outside a Christian perspective, it sure gets a bit weird, doesn't it?) This rite is supposed to honor and invoke the power of when Jesus supposedly performed this ritual at the Last Supper. That act in itself harkens back to the practice of animal sacrifice, one of the most famous being the lamb that Abraham sacrificed to Yahweh in place of his son Isaac (with the okay from that god, of course). This rite is a strange evolution of sacrifice that can be performed only by ordained priests and no one else.

I was drawn to the altar as a small child. Both of my brothers did their time as altar boys, and I didn't understand why it was okay for them to be up there but not me. (In the parishes we belonged to, female acolytes were not a thing until after I reached adulthood.) During a first grade field trip to the church (not during an actual mass), I snuck up there and sat in one of the chairs designated for the priests and acolytes. That earned me a trip to the principal's office to see Sister Margaret—on my birthday, no less. Ironically, that memory is also tied to my experience a short time later of that same nun giving me a large laminated artwork of a unicorn on a mountain—one that was far better than most of the 1980s-style unicorn art of the time!

With my altar aspirations dashed, I turned my attention to the darker, less-celebrated corners of the church—the places where the old women in my grandparents' church gathered to pray, light candles, and tend to the vases of flowers for the saints. The job of saints, according to Catholic belief, is to act as intermediaries between us lowly beings and God. There in those dark, quiet corners of the church, you could look into the eyes of the saints (or, in the case of Saint Lucy, directly at the eyeballs on the plate in her hands) without needing anyone's permission to communicate and interact with them. In these places you could build a relationship with the saints— one candle, one prayer, one vase of flowers, or one dusting at a time—and, in turn, connect with God. They were accessible.

But that's not the only place where the saints resided. Away from the church, in the kitchens, bedrooms, and foyers of my maternal relatives, you could find more images of the saints. Sure, there was the occasional crucifix or thorn-encrusted bust of Jesus, but there were more statues and framed pictures of the Virgin Mary and any number of patron saints. Nearby would be candles, bud vases with fresh herbs or flowers, miraculous medals and special jewelry, and other special tokens. Every evening my grandfather would lay his wallet and keys on a dish in front of a saint on his dresser. He would make sure the statue of Mary in the backyard was always clean and had beautiful flowers surrounding her.

I also know of many an Italian aunt, mother, or grandmother who would keep a little satchel (often red) in her bosom or handbag. Depending on the lady, it might contain her rosaries and/or a mixture of protective charms and medals, a sprig of herbs or dried flowers, and other talismans— items that could be held, prayed over, and kept for safety, luck, and other blessings.

Now, you're probably wondering, what does all this talk about Catholicism have to do with Witchcraft? Isn't this a book about the Witch's altar? Actually, practices we culturally inherit or grow up with can have a lot to do with how we view altars, worship, ritual, and other practices. I think it's important to consider how these things can influence our own paths. Many people find the path of the Witch while coming from other faiths, and it can take a very long time to unload the baggage we may carry from them. Often, without meaning to, we carry certain notions of how things should and shouldn't be, because we're still using the building blocks of a previous spirituality as our guide. We may still have certain prejudices about who can do what in a ritual and who can talk to the divine, as well as latent taboos about sexuality, cleanliness, and other things. We may also continue doing certain things because they feel familiar to us, and find creative ways to justify our actions without considering the source.

For example, when I was a young Witchlet on my path, one of the common myths that was being passed around was that Christianity stole much of its practices from Pagans. In fact, I still see this claim circulating on the internet. Now, I will say that if we consider the subject of overlapping sacred places—where churches were built over Pagan temples, sacred springs, etc.—yes, there are some good arguments to be made for coopting. We'll talk about that more later on in the book. Just remember that Christianity is a relative newcomer in a long list of religions that have absorbed or reused previously determined sacred places.

The Wiccan rite of cakes and ale, in particular, could be linked with Holy Communion, based on some creative theories—especially in the work of Margaret Murray. But it's very hard to reconstruct accurate practices based on forced confessions, as it's quite likely that witch hunters and clergymen purposely distorted Christian practices to inspire horror in the public. Under the duress of torture, people will admit to anything, especially as they're being force-fed tales of horrific atrocities. Second, in the larger scheme of things, all religions do one of two things: either they borrow heavily from the systems that predate them, or they devise something on the opposite end of the spectrum. As human beings, we love food and drink—we celebrate with it, and we use it for offerings and sacrifices because it has innate value. We would be hard-pressed to find any culture that doesn't have some sort of ceremony or ritual that doesn't involve food and/or beverages. The best thing we can do is take the time to consider what has meaning for us personally, and choose practices that make sense for our own paths.

Another lesson I learned through my experience as a Catholic is that you don't have to be an ordained clergy member performing a high-ritual act in order to make use of an altar. Even "lay" people can connect with the sacred through everyday tasks and in ordinary places. It doesn't have to happen in a formally sanctioned and designated place or building, nor do you need anyone else to act as an intermediary between you and the gods. As a Modern Traditional Witch, I believe that we're innately a part of the divine and can speak directly with the gods—no intermediary needed. In fact, most of the time when I'm interacting with gods and spirits, I could be anywhere—in bed, driving, or out in the woods.

Reflect on your past and what has influenced you when considering how you would like to make and use altars. What do you personally believe and feel to be true? What do you wish to explore more deeply in your practice? What happens at an altar? Who can make an altar? Who can use an altar? Why build an altar in the first place? Should it be a permanent fixture or something temporary or portable?

Human beings are wired to communicate: we build, we talk, we draw, we sing, we make music, we write. Altars are another extension of the communication process. Who are we communicating with at an altar? There are endless possibilities. Most commonly, altars are built in honor of gods, but there are other purposes for them too. They can be created to help us remember the dead and our ancestors, to recognize the seasons and sacred days, to be a source of inspiration for a talent, to be a focused site for spellcraft and/or divination, to commemorate an occasion or event, to honor the spirit of a place, to be an anchor, or to mark a special location, place of transition, or border. We can even build altars to help us connect with ourselves.

So while we can argue semantics about which term fits what space the best, for the purpose of this book we'll use the word *altar* for both general and specific spaces. Whether you're thinking of building a shrine, sanctuary, tabernacle, or temple, the goal here is to focus on the practice and application of sacred space. We seek to challenge what you think an altar should look like, and open you to more possibilities that will enhance your personal practice. An altar can reside within a matchbox, or it can be an entire room. It can travel with you, or it can be part of a permanent installation. Altars can be entirely human-made, inspired by nature, or made of the elements themselves. What unifies them all is the altar maker's desire to communicate, to connect, and to interact. Perhaps that's what truly makes an altar an altar. Keep this in mind as we explore all the aspects of the altar together.

Tip: Avoid Confusing *Altar* with *Alter*

One of the most common spelling mistakes I see is confusing *altar* with *alter*. Quite simply, an *altar* is a noun—it's a place. On the other hand, *alter* is a verb meaning to change, modify, or make different. One easy way to remember the difference between the two is to link the word *altar* with the noun *activity*, remembering that they both have an *a*. Activities happen at the altar. To relate *alter* to another word, connect it with the verb *evolve*, remembering the *e* in each word. To alter something is to cause it to evolve.

LTAR-NATIVES

Altar Reflections

IN MY WORK of connecting to the inner sacred landscape of self, the altar is the second conduit between that numinous realm and the shared reality. The first conduit is the practitioner, in all our imperfection and grace.

We keep our records at the altar; we connect to our body, our heart, and our mind here. The altar is the sticking place where we screw our courage, and is sometimes the place where our courage gets screwed. Intense and personal magickal work can be scary!

The altar is a bridge that leads to the wild wonder that dwells in each of us. It exists in both realms and holds objects, thoughts, and visions gathered on one side or another; it reminds us that our actions in either place bear fruit in all places. Integrity is paramount.

We consider the altar as an ally in our journeys; it's a place and a thing, but also a person, with a spirit of its own. My altar is an antique vanity, with a huge round mirror, several drawers, and different levels. She has mismatched pulls, and the silver is mottled so that there are spots in the reflection. She is old and beautiful, warm and inviting. When we were moving, she ended up in storage for several months. When I got her back and into my studio, it was like a pall had been lifted and my magick was stronger than ever. I love her dearly.

She is her own entity, and at the same time, as a place, she provides a gathering spot for other spirits. These spirits may be bodied (as in a stone, plant, or candle) or unbodied (as in ancestors or other guides). Spells live here, as do images of the gods I work with, along with my deep well of compassion. She is the address I give to those powers I want to connect with; they know they can find me at the home of my magick, my charming and adept altar.

Jenya T. Beachy
Jenya T. Beachy is the author of *The Secret Country of Yourself: Discover the Powerful Magic of Your Endless Inner World* (Llewellyn, 2017). She writes, teaches, and performs other arcane magicks amongst the strawberry fields near the coast of Central California.

CHAPTER TWO

The Altar in History
& Other Traditions
(Jason)

Altars are probably some of the oldest religious tools in history. The moment someone placed a spiritual object on a large rock or tree stump, they were utilizing an altar. Just *how old* altars might be depends on when one believes religion first came into the world. Since our earliest ancestors did not leave a written legacy, constructing the early millennia of religious history requires a lot of guesswork.

Modern human beings (*Homo sapiens*) have only been around for about 200,000 years, but some of our more distant ancestors could have been practicing something religious (and possibly using an altar) hundreds of thousands of years before we emerged on the scene. Though *Homo erectus* (our immediate forebears) were incapable of speech as we think of it today, this species was able to establish a pretty sophisticated existence as a hunter-gatherer society, complete with tools and homemade shelters.

In addition to those technologies, *Homo erectus* were also using red ochre for some sort of decorative or spiritual reason. Red ochre is a compound with no real use other than to color objects red. Could red have had some sort of spiritual significance in ancient society? Some scholars think so and believe that religious ritual would be the natural end result of such beliefs. If *Homo erectus* were participating in some sort of ritual one million years ago, they probably would have needed to set that red ochre somewhere…like on an altar. It's where we put our stuff.

While such theories are tantalizing, they are hard to prove with any certainty. When researching ancient history, what matters most are physical objects, and one of the most amazing objects comes from Chauvet Cave in southern France. It's at Chauvet where we find overwhelming evidence of the world's first altar.

Chauvet is one of the many painted caves that have been found throughout modern-day France, Portugal, and Spain, known to most of us because of the vivid and striking animal images painted and carved on their walls. Chauvet was one of the first cave systems to be painted by humans, and some of the images that adorn its walls are 30,000 years old. But the most intriguing thing about Chauvet is not the images on the walls, but the altar that has existed there for most of that time.

In one of the cave rooms at Chauvet sits a rock that most likely fell from the ceiling directly into the center of the room. Surrounding that rock are forty-five bear skulls, and a forty-sixth skull that sits upon the rock. This is very likely the world's first knowable altar.

No one is exactly certain what went on in the bear room at Chauvet, though it must have been something deliberate. The only bones in the room are the bear skulls, so those skulls must have had a specific significance, more so than a leg or pelvis bone. It's possible that someone simply picked bear skulls up off the ground and placed them on and around the rock in the center of the room, but I find that doubtful. It's more likely that the skulls were brought into the room because the rock created a natural altar and it was decided that at least one of the skulls should be off the ground to capture the eye. Under the skull-on-the-rock are scorch marks, indicating the presence of fire on top of the rock before the skull was set there. Could this be further proof that this particular rock was used as an altar?

The Altar in History & Other Traditions

Humans did something spiritual in the caves of Europe continuously for over 16,000 years, but with the exception of the bear altar at Chauvet there are no other altars associated with the caves. To find the next altar in history we must go to Turkey and the temple at Göbekli Tepe, the world's first human-made spiritual center. Built over 11,600 years ago, Göbekli Tepe is older than Stonehenge and the pyramids of Egypt, and existed before agriculture.

Göbekli Tepe was constructed as a series of rings, culminating in two large T-shaped pillars in its center. The pillars are thought to be representative of human beings (perhaps a revered ancestor), are ornately decorated, and weigh up to sixteen tons! (This accomplishment is even more impressive when one considers that these pillars were created with nothing more than chisels and muscle.) The center-ring pillars sit on a large stone platform that most likely served as a place for offerings. This would make the pillars a very early altar.

A more proper altar was unearthed in present-day Bulgaria in 2004. At about 8,000 years old, it might be Europe's first sacrificial altar. Stairs lead down to a cylindrical altar area where offerings of grain were left, perhaps in order to ensure a successful harvest. The people who built this early altar were among the first farmers in Europe, and as agriculture became more common in the ancient world, so did religion and altars.

Altars in the Ancient World

Long before I identified as a Witch, I was captivated by Greek mythology, and when I had to make a clay art project during my freshman year of high school, I decided to make a temple to the goddess Aphrodite. My temple was simple, with three malformed columns in the front, three walls, and a roof. In the center of my clay temple I constructed an altar to the goddess, where I envisioned myself leaving her offerings. My offerings to Aphrodite were generally tiny objects I constructed out of clay or perhaps a spare coin. While my altar was a mostly innocent place, altars in ancient Greece were much different.

The idea of animal sacrifice feels problematic to many of us today, and it's not something I generally see practiced in any Wiccan-Witchcraft circles. But to our ancestors, animal sacrifice was a common enough occurrence and was often practiced directly on or above an altar. Blood from sacrificed animals was then collected and spread over the top of the altar and its sides. Staining the altar with blood (known in Greek as *splanchna*) was considered a dutiful religious act.

After the sacrifice, the animal was butchered, with the portion going to the gods burned directly on the altar itself. The gods were generally given the less desirable parts of the sacrificed animal, with the best bits eaten by worshipers. Sacrifice may also have served as a type of charity, feeding poorer citizens who otherwise would have been unable to ever eat a meat dinner. The exception to this was a holocaust (and yes, that's where the modern word comes from), a special observance where the entire animal was given to the god being sacrificed to.

Greek altar

Fire was such an important part of Greek religious life that ancient Greek altars contained a hearth, with many of the fires in those hearths continually attended to. Because of this, Greek religious scholar Walter Burkert, in his book *Greek Religion*, called the altar the "pre-eminent fire place, the hearth of the gods" (Burkert, 61). Offerings such as wine, oil, and cakes were also burned in such altars, animal sacrifice being more the exception than the general rule in ancient Greece.

The Greeks generally constructed altars out of large slabs of rock, and out of brick in the larger and more sophisticated temples. In some places altars grew organically out of the bone and ash left at the end of a sacrifice. The Altar of Zeus at Pergamon was said to be made only of such materials, allowed to pile up over the years until they formed a great mound. Altars were the centerpiece of ancient Greek religion, and were often ornately decorated to reflect that reverence. When the Greeks worshiped their gods in the temple, the altar was the centerpiece of their devotion.

Interestingly, the Mycenaean and Minoan civilizations that predated the Greeks did not kindle fires upon their altars or leave the remains of sacrificed animals upon them. Altars were used to hold devotional items, but the whole enterprise was much cleaner than the later Greek version.

The Greeks were not alone in their use of the altar as a place for sacrifices, but not all altars in the ancient world were used for such endeavors. The Roman religion, with its emphasis on both a public and a private cult, utilized sacrificial altars in its public temples and private altars for home worship. A *lararium* (the Roman name for a home altar) was the centerpiece of Roman family life, and a place where Romans could

The Altar in History & Other Traditions

directly interact with their gods, household spirits, and the house *genius* (a sort of spirit guaranteeing the continued existence of the family). Lorariums were sometimes just a niche in the wall or a picture on the wall of the household deities, and for richer families something more resembling a modern Witch's altar.

ALTAR-NATIVES
The Altar in Heathenry

DESPITE THE DIVERSITY of approaches to the practice of modern Heathenry, one of the things adherents of the religion generally agree upon is the setup of the ritual altar. The two main rituals Heathens practice are *blót* and *sumbel*; the former is a ceremonial "sacrifice" in which offerings are made, and the latter a drinking ritual consisting of three rounds dedicated to the gods/goddesses, ancestors/heroes, and personal boasts/oaths. The altar is a dedicated surface on which the implements for these rituals are stored and displayed.

Accounts of altars from antiquity in the primary sources of Norse/Germanic myth depict them as places of literal sacrifice. For example, in stanza 10 of the thirteenth-century Prose Edda's *Song of Hyndla*, the goddess Freya recounts the virtues of her companion Ottar (Larrington, 254). In doing so, she

commends his dedication to her by praising the altar he constructed in her name:

> He's made an altar for me, faced with stone,
>   now that stone has turned to glass;
> he's reddened the new altar with ox blood,
>   Ottar has always trusted in the Asynior.

Therein is the clear implication that it is Ottar's depend-
able sacrificing to her that has gained him her respect. The
takeaway here is that although there are still modern Heathen
groups that perform literal sacrifice during blót as did Ottar, it
isn't so much what's offered but rather the magnitude of the
concept of reciprocity that is paramount. It is for this reason
that the maxim "a gift for a gift" is so widely used amongst
Heathens in and out of ritual. To gain favor with the gods/
goddesses, something should be given to them in return, left
upon the altar if corporeal.

In the *Dictionary of Northern Mythology*, Rudolf Simek says
that "there appear to have been two types of altar for sacrifices
and for other cult activities, either a simple heap of stones
(*horgr*), or cult frame made of wood," which was known as
stalli (Simek, 11). Such altars may have been housed within
a temple (*hof*) or shrine (*vé*). It is thought that the wooden
frame may have acted "as shelter for the idols...within"
(Simek, 156). Additionally there is evidence in sources such

as Kjalnesinga saga of oath-rings and offering bowls being present upon the altar platform. Items found on the modern Asatru/Heathen altar derive from such sources.

Most modern Heathens use libations such as beer or mead (or something nonalcoholic for minors and those who abstain) as symbolic substitutes for the blood sacrifices of yore. A drinking horn is therefore one of the staple items on the altar. Other items include the aforementioned oath-ring and offering bowl (to pour libation into) and some form of representation (a painting, statue, etc.) of the deity being honored. In many cases there is also an ancestor plate upon which offerings are left during the post-ritual feast. Some groups keep a Thor's hammer upon the altar, both as a symbol of the faith and, in some cases, as a consecratory tool.

Dave Iverson
Dave Iverson lives in Massachusetts with his wife Lynn, son Tor, daughter Lilac, and two German shepherd dogs Freki and Freya. He is a high school English teacher and a longtime Ásatrúar and member of Raven Kindred North.

From Altars of Fire to the Witch's Altar

The texts known as the *Greek Magical Papyri* are the ancient world's closest parallel to modern Witchcraft. The papyri are a series of magickal spells and operations designed for a variety of purposes, from restraining anger to attracting love.

They also include various instructions for calling to deity, along with complex spellwork that often calls for an altar. The papyri were popular from about 200 BCE to 400 CE, and contain Christian, Jewish, and ancient pagan ideas and concepts. They were not a single book or manual, but a series of individual spells that seem to represent the same tradition.

In the papyri, the altar itself is utilized as a magickal tool specifically, with some spells calling for altars made of wood, earth, or vine wood. Perhaps my favorite set of instructions for a specific altar are for a spell calling for a *pure altar*, which is apparently made of "two unbaked bricks" formed into four horn-shaped items, upon which is laid "fruit-bearing branches." Altars in the papyri are also places for holding ritual tools, such as incense and salt, along with sacrificial fires, but they represent a clear step forward in the development of magickal altars.

It's in the Middle Ages with the development of modern ceremonial magick that we begin to encounter altars that we might truly recognize as being similar to our own. Beginning in the thirteenth century with the translation of the Arabic *Picatrix* into Spanish and lasting into the present day, ceremonial magick and the grimoires it inspired have been a tremendous influence on modern Witchcraft. The most influential European grimoire, the *Key of Solomon* (sometimes known as the *Clavicula Salomonis*), doesn't use the word *altar* once in its text, but the *idea* of the altar looms over the entire work.

The magick in the *Key* is generally focused on creating certain talismanic pentacles to use in various magickal operations. To make the pentacles described in the text requires a great deal of pre-ritual prep work, followed by several grueling magickal procedures. Due to the complexity of the work, the *Key* requires a closet's worth of tools, including nine variations on the knife and/or sword, along with two wands and various other implements, such as salt, the pentacle, candle flame, and incense. Having an altar for all these tools is the only logical recourse for the resourceful magician.

The German theologian Henry Cornelius Agrippa calls the magician's altar "holy" in his highly influential *Three Books of Occult Philosophy* (1533). Agrippa also says that altars (among many other things) require a "supreme and special reverence and comeliness" (Agrippa, 669). Agrippa, much like the writer of the *Key of Solomon* before him, rarely mentions the altar, but it's obvious that the work must center around something, and that something is what we could call an altar.

In the late nineteenth century, the English organization the Hermetic Order of the Golden Dawn changed the face of ceremonial magick by creating a ritual structure inspired by many of its most influential texts. In doing so they also helped simplify ceremonial magick by cutting down on the number of tools needed to practice it. Their altar, and the working tools upon it, would go on to influence most modern forms of Witchcraft.

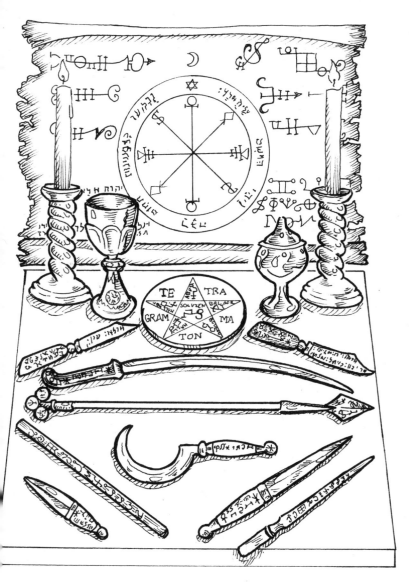

Tools from the Key of Solomon

A list of essential items needed to practice Golden Dawn–style magick includes the group's symbol (a red cross in or above a white triangle), two candles, a chalice of water, incense, a ceremonial blade (such as a dagger), a wand, and a black altar. In many ways the Golden Dawn created the modern magickal altar by utilizing a relatively easy setup and stocking it with tools that could be readily acquired. (One blade is much easier to obtain than the nine required by the *Key of Solomon*.) The relatively small number of tools also helped to dictate the size of the work altar being used to something more like the end tables many of us use today.

The first modern Witchcraft book to mention the altar was Gerald Gardner's *Witchcraft Today* (1954). Gardner doesn't write much about the altar in *Today*, but he does mention it as the "central point" that Witch ritual revolves around. A poem that appears a bit later in the book (chapter 13) lists the altar as one of the Witch's central tools, and instructs that "Flaming Censers on the sweet altar, light." In his 1959 book *The Meaning of Witchcraft*, Gardner includes a picture of a Witch's altar. Not surprisingly, it resembles what many Witches use today.

By the 1970s, the first full books of Witch ritual were being published, and not surprisingly they mentioned the altar, along with Witchcraft's other most often used tools. The *Grimoire of Lady Sheba* (who was born Jessie Wicker Bell, 1920–

2002) doesn't have much to say about altars (or anything else, really), but it does feature two photos of Sheba's altar, which serves to emphasize how important a good working altar is.

Scott Cunningham's 1989 book *Wicca: A Guide for the Solitary Practitioner* was the first Witch book to talk about the altar at length, and even included a suggested altar layout (a first in a Witchcraft book, as far as I can tell). Since then, nearly every Witchcraft book on the market has included at least a little something about the altar, a trend that seems likely to continue.

ALTAR-NATIVES

*New Orleans Voodoo Altars:
To Infinity and Beyond*

IN THE RELIGION of New Orleans Voodoo, altars and shrines can contain just about anything. They are seen as sacred repositories of *ashe*, the divine energy of the universe.

Most often altars contain candles, incense, images, and offerings for the *lwa*, the gods and goddesses of the religion. Like everything else in the city, Voodoo draws its components from the multicultural environment around it. New Orleans is home to a diverse population that stems from its history as a colony of France, Spain, and England. While the city is classified as part of the Southern United States, some have argued that, with its high level of diversity, it is another country.

The images that you will find on a New Orleans Voodoo altar are very often Catholic ones. The guardian of the cross-roads, Papa Legba (or Papa Lebat), is frequently represented by Saint Peter. This is an example of religious syncretism, the process wherein one culture uses the symbols of another. Slavery and oppression made these representations a necessity, as African traditional religious practices were outlawed. The use of Catholic imagery allowed worshipers to honor and salute their heritage with a reduced risk of punishment, but the use of these mainstream items is more complicated than that. If we examine the image of Saint Peter, we see the presence of keys. This is to represent Peter's role as the gate-keeper to heaven. Because of this role, Peter is associated with the ashe, or divine energy, of Papa Legba. Thus Saint Peter is shown on altars, along with the other ritual items for Legba, which include keys, coffee, etc.

New Orleans Voodoo also uses ritual symbols known as *veves* as part of their altars. Many say these symbols grew from the ground drawings left in the dirt after ritual. People noticed that after certain ceremonies, symbols would be left on the ground from people and animals walking and dancing on the space. They began to recreate these symbols in cornmeal or flour at the beginning of a ceremony as temporary portals to honor and attract the lwa. Over time these symbols began to be created as sequin flags, iron sculptures, and more. Today these symbols and the artwork created featuring them are a common sight on altars.

Another common altar item is a *govi*, or soul jar. These are crafted with natural items to hold and honor the ashe of an individual. Govis are placed on the altar by mutual arrangement between practitioners and the lwa.

New Orleans Voodoo altars also contain food, drink, money, and other items of significance. While respect is paramount, and things are placed mindfully and purposefully, there is almost nothing that is across-the-board forbidden to place on an altar. Do bear in mind, however, that all offerings should be left under the guidance and care of the mambo or houngan (priestess or priest) of the hounfor (temple).

Lilith Dorsey

Lilith has been practicing magick since 1991 and is the editor/publisher of *Oshun-African Magickal Quarterly*, a filmmaker, and the author of *Love Magic* (2016, Weiser Books) and *Voodoo and Afro-Caribbean Paganism* (2005, Citadel Press). She has also worked as a choreographer and dancer for jazz legend Dr. John's "Night Tripper" Voodoo show.

LTAR-NATIVES

The Traditional Witch's Altar

WITHIN THE REALM of traditional Witchcraft, one of the primary, and arguably most beloved, ritual tools is the forked staff known as the *stang*. In its simplest form, the stang is a bifurcated branch, traditionally of ash wood, shod with an iron nail. However, there are many variations, including staffs topped with animal horns/antlers and even old pitchforks.

While there exist various old woodcuts depicting Witches making use of forked branches, the stang itself appears to be of a more modern vintage. In fact, it is Robert Cochrane, the famed Traditional Witch of the 1960s, who is largely credited with its creation and implementation. He described the stang as being the "supreme implement," which is only fitting considering the many functions it serves in magical practice. For example, today many Witches use this tool for directing their power and for aiding in hedge-crossing. However, the primary occupation of the stang is as an altar and a symbolic representation of the Horned One.

As an altar, the stang is commonly placed at the northern point of the compass (or ritual space), as this is the direction long associated with the Horned One. Like any other altar, the stang is often adorned with various symbolic objects, depending upon the time of year and the nature of the ritual at hand.

For example, it is traditional to hang a garland of different foliage upon the stang as a representation of the shifting seasonal tides. A pair of crossed arrows are hung with the garland, emblematic of the dual aspects of the Horned One as the light-bearing God of life and the dark, chthonic Lord of the Mound. In addition, it is common for a candle to be placed between the tines of the stang as a representation of the "light betwixt the horns," or the divine inspiration granted by the Old One. Any other items needed for the ritual working, such as offerings, are usually placed around the base of the stang.

If you're interested in incorporating the stang into your own practice, the recommended route would be to craft your own. You can do this either by going out and finding a forked branch or by procuring a pitchfork. In the case of sourcing a branch, consider the inherent virtues of different trees, and which aligns best with your intentions. Next, no matter if you take a fallen branch or cut a live one, make sure to thank the spirits and give appropriate offerings. Then get creative, striping, sanding, inscribing, and staining your stang as desired. The final step is to hallow your new ritual tool, infusing it with your cunning will and dedicating it to the service of the Horned One.

Kelden

Kelden is a Traditional Witch, writer, and avid gardener living in northern Minnesota.

CHAPTER THREE

The Pentacle
(Jason)

It seems a little odd to be including a chapter on the pentacle in a book about altars, but in many ways the pentacle is like "the altar on the altar." It's the one Witch tool that I actively set other tools and magickal objects upon (just like with an altar), and as my practice has deepened over the years I find myself more and more drawn to it.

The pentacle is often confused with the pentagram, and according to the Oxford English Dictionary, *pentacle* is a synonym for *pentagram*, but that's not how the words are generally used in Witchcraft. In Witchcraft, the word *pentagram* refers to a five-pointed star, with the single point usually facing upward. Pentagrams are often ringed by a circle touching all five points of the star, but the circle is not necessary for something to be called a pentagram.

The word *pentacle* most often refers to a disc-shaped working tool generally out of metal, clay, or wood with a star in the center. The center star tends to have five points, though variations do appear from time to time and vary from Witch to Witch. A pentagram charm on a necklace is often called a pentacle too, which makes sense because just like the working tool, it's a physical object generally made of metal, clay, or wood.

Both *pentagram* and *pentacle* come from the Greek word *pentagrammon*, *penta* being Greek for "five" (think pentagon) and *grammon* meaning "line." Pentacle first came into the English language during the sixteenth century and originally referred to any magickal disc used to summon angels or demons (generally referred to as "spirits" in the books of the period). Most often these discs contained five-pointed stars, but not always. The sixteenth-century *Key of Solomon*, for example, provides instructions for creating forty-four different pentacles, only two of which contain a five-pointed star.

The word *pentagram* has only been in use since the nineteenth century, but pentagrams as we understand them today have a long history in religious and magickal tradition. Five-pointed stars were used in ancient Greece, Sumer, Babylon, India, China, Mexico, and Peru. The pentagram was later used in Christian tradition to represent the five wounds of Christ upon the cross, and for good luck. The device also appeared on the shield of the legendary Sir Gawain of King Arthur's

Round Table. In Jewish tradition the five-pointed star can be seen in the Kabbalah, and there are claims that it was also used as the seal for the city of Jerusalem.

Ceramic pentacle, pentagram in the middle

To the followers of the Greek Pythagoras, the five-pointed star was valued for its mathematical precision and because it was said to represent the five points of the human body: head, arms, and legs. A similar idea was expressed by Henry Cornelius Agrippa in his *Second Book of Occult Philosophy* (1533).

Agrippa's use of the symbol made it forever synonymous with Western magickal traditions and, by extension, modern Witchcraft. Other contemporary groups to use the pentagram include the Freemasons and the Church of Jesus Christ of Latter-day Saints.

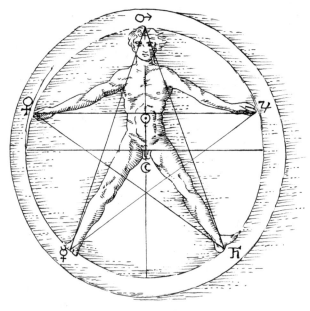

Vitruvian Man

In modern Witchcraft the pentagram right-side up is said to represent the triumph of the spiritual over the material.

The upward point represents spirit, with the other four points representing water, fire, earth, and air when listed clockwise. The upside-down pentagram is often associated with Satanic or left-hand-path traditions, and was popularized for this purpose in the 1960s by the founder of the Church of Satan, Anton LaVey (1930–1997), because it represented the triumph of the material over the spiritual. In some Wiccan traditions the upside-down pentacle represents a Witch elevated to the second degree, a representation that predates LaVey's church.

What Is a Pentacle Used For?

Most Witch books that include the pentacle say very little about it. Generally it's listed as an element of earth, and as something used to consecrate salt, water, incense, and candles. Those things are true, but they downplay the pentacle's original meaning and significance in circle. In *Witchcraft Today*, Gerald Gardner writes that the "unimportant pentacle" was said "to be used to command spirits," though he points out that most Witches don't generally "command" spirits or other sentient forces.

Gardner's thoughts on the pentacle in *Witchcraft Today* are valuable because they shed light on the pentacle's true function in the modern Craft. Certainly the pentacle is used for consecrating and charging items, but its original use was as a tool to call upon otherworldly entities. Beginning in the Renaissance and continuing through the early twentieth century, these entities were variously described as spirits, demons, or angels. Many Witches still work with such beings, but many more of us work with deities: goddesses, gods, and everything in between. The pentacle is not just a tool used for consecrating things, it's a window between the worlds (and we can open it!).

I often think of the pentacle as my altar's "umbilical cord," as it's what connects my ritual space to powers much greater and higher than myself. When I was a fetus, my mother was the higher power, and now as an adult I honor the higher powers of the Lord and Lady through the pentacle. If a magick circle is a "space between the worlds," it makes sense that there would be some sort of gateway into that other world on our altars.

In ritual the gods don't just suddenly emerge for the pentacles on our altars, but I do feel as if that's where a great deal of power and energy radiate from, which is probably the reason the pentacle is used for charging and consecrating items. When blessing the elements in ritual (usually represented by water, salt, incense, and a lit candle), each individual "element" is put upon the pentacle for consecration. I think most Witches simply place things on the pentacle without wondering why, but we set things on the pentacle because it's a bridge between the worlds. It's a place radiating power, and it's holy because the gods exist just on the other side of it. It's for this reason that many Witches also place magickal items on their pentacles to charge.

Ceremonial magicians sometimes refer to a personal pentacle as a *pantacle* (because it contains the word *pan*, which translates to "everything" or "all" in Greek). Unlike the traditional pentacle, the pantacle is an extremely personal tool. It's designed to represent how the individual magician understands the entire universe and their place within it. Pantacles often include a magician's magickal motto, a phrase designed to emphasize the magickal nature of the practitioner. I like the idea of a very personal pentacle, though I don't think I've ever met another Witch who uses the word pantacle when talking about their ritual tools.

Symbols on the Pentacle

Pentacles by their very nature have always had a variety of symbols inscribed upon them. Even in Witchcraft it's acceptable to forgo the usual five-pointed star in the pentacle's center and replace it with something else. For example, a Witch with a strong connection to the English occultist Aleister Crowley and the O.T.O. (Ordo Templi Orientis) might replace the pentagram with the unicursal hexagram, a six-pointed symbol generally with a small flower in the middle. Many in the Anderson Feri Tradition of Witchcraft identify with the septagram, a seven-pointed star, which is another option. Such variances are not common but are certainly valid ones to make, depending on what each individual Witch resonates with.

Far more common than alternatives to the five-pointed star are additional symbols generally placed around the outside edges of the pentacle. Those symbols tend to represent the traditions and beliefs of the particular Witch (or coven) who chose to place them on their pentacle. Many of the most popular pentacle symbols have been in general use since at least the 1950s, with some going back hundreds of years to the grimoire tradition and other varieties of magickal practice.

When it comes to extra symbols, there are no right or wrong ones. If something calls to you, it's perfectly acceptable to place it on your pentacle. Symbols such as runes or the ogham alphabet are other alternatives and can be used to spell out an idea (such as "As above, so below") or the name of a particular deity close to the individual Witch. Astrological symbols are another option that would be welcome on any pentacle (especially the symbol of your birth sign on a personal pentacle). In the course of writing this book, I purchased a new pentacle that contained the phases of the moon on its outside edge. When I use it during ritual, I rotate it so the current moon phase is represented at the top of the pentacle.

Many of the more common sets of symbols found on pentacles today tend to represent deity (the Goddess and God being most common), the Witch's working tools (which often have elemental associations), the changing of the seasons, and the elements of earth, air, fire, and water. Here are some of the more common symbols that I've seen on pentacles over the years, or that grace one of the pentacles I'm currently using.

	Goddess symbol: A circle flanked by two crescent moons is a traditional symbol of the Goddess in Wicca.
	Goddess symbol (2): This is an "abbreviation" of the previous symbol that is particularly useful if you don't have a lot of space on your pentacle.
	God symbol: A circle with a crescent moon (for horns) is a traditional symbol of the God in Wicca.
	Horned God symbol: Similar to the God symbol, the Horned God symbol is much clearer about the horns.

	Upside-down triangle: This is a symbol for the first degree in some initiatory traditions of Wiccan-Witchcraft. Degree symbols are common on the pentacle.
	Upside-down pentagram: This is the symbol of the second degree in some traditions. Because of the negative associations of the upside-down pentagram in popular culture, it's not used all that often today.
	Pentagram with triangle: This is the symbol of the third degree in some traditions. Another way of representing this symbol is simply to place a point-up triangle directly above your pentacle's pentagram.
	Wheel of the Year symbol: This is representative of the eight great sabbats present in most Witchcraft traditions.
	Air symbol: An upward-pointing triangle with a line in the middle represents the element of air.

	Earth symbol: A downward-pointing triangle with a line in the middle represents the element of earth.
	Water symbol: Triangles are popular in Witchcraft. A downward-pointing triangle for the element of water is identical to the symbol of the first degree.
	Fire symbol: Fire can be represented with a plain upward-pointing triangle. I'd probably pass on the element symbols if I were placing the degree symbols on my pentacle.
	Triquetra: The triquetra is extremely popular in many Wiccan circles today and is generally seen as representative of the Triple Goddess or Wicca as a whole.
	Tree of Life: Interpretations of the Tree of Life differ from Witch to Witch. This symbol tends to remind me of the infinite and my connection to the natural world.

	Athame: One of the most common working tools, the athame is often associated with fire and sometimes air.
	Wand: Nothing says magick like a wand. It's generally associated with the element of air and sometimes fire.
	Broom: The broom is representative of the earth element and is used to purify the circle before ritual.
	Chalice: The chalice is a symbol of the water element and can also serve as a symbol of abundance due to its association with wine.
	Cauldron: Witches use cauldrons for a variety of reasons, and they are one of the tools most connected with Witchcraft.

In addition to the symbols included here, many Witches like to decorate their pentacles with symbols relating to the seasons. Examples of this include a pumpkin for autumn, a snowflake for winter, blooming flowers in the spring, and a green leaf in the summer. There are also more stylized symbols for each season depending on which book one consults, but I much prefer the personal touch of adding symbols I associate with the turning of the Wheel of the Year.

Making Your Own Pentacle

While the pentacle is one of the most important tools in modern Witchcraft, it's not particularly easy to just go out and buy one at your local Witch or metaphysical shop or even online. The local stores in my area have all sorts of athames, cauldrons, deity statues, and candles for sale, but rarely a pentacle suitable for ritual. Luckily, the pentacle is the easiest tool to make yourself.

The simplest homemade pentacle requires just four tools: a pencil, a pen or marker, a ruler, and a paper plate. Yup, you can make a perfectly acceptable pentacle for under twenty-five cents! Using your ruler and pencil, simply mark out a reasonably good-looking pentagram onto your plate. Once you've got it set up to your satisfaction, go over the pencil lines with a pen or marker, and voila! There it is, an instant pentacle. With a little hard work and some fancy coloring, a paper-plate pentacle can even end up looking kind of stylish.

If a paper-plate pentacle doesn't sound witchy enough, it's also easy enough to make one using a ceramic plate. Nearly every chain or discount store sells some type of one-color dinner or dessert/salad plate, and they make great pentacles! It requires a few extra steps than for a paper-plate pentacle, but it's still easy enough to create for the artistically uninclined.

First you'll need to determine how large you want the pentagram you'll be placing in the center of your plate to be. I generally suggest situating the pentagram on the flat part of the plate, leaving the outer raised edge of the plate empty (and this comes in handy if you want to add symbols to your pentacle later). If you're using a small plate, you can print out a suitably sized pentagram from your computer. If your plate is larger, you'll probably have to create one on your own.

After you've printed or drawn a pentagram that's the correct size for your plate, take a sheet of tracing paper and make a copy of it with a pencil. Once you have your tracing, set it down in the center of your plate where you'd like it to be and go over the tracing with a pencil, pushing down reasonably hard. The graphite from the pencil should bleed through the tracing paper onto the plate, giving you a rough outline of a pentagram that you can then make permanent in a variety of ways.

The easiest way to create a long-lasting pentagram design is with a Sharpie marker. Simply go over your pencil pentagram with whatever color of Sharpie appeals to you, and instant pentacle! To make your work last even longer, wait for the marker ink to dry and then bake your plate in a 350°F oven for at least thirty minutes. This will make the design(s) on your plate close to permanent and even safe to eat off! The only downside to the Sharpie-on-a-plate method is that the design is not dishwasher-safe.

Another variation on the drawn-on ceramic plate is to substitute acrylic paint for the Sharpie ink. Pretty much everything else in the operation is the same: measure your pentagram, get it onto tracing paper, and then use the tracing paper to create an outline. However, instead of drawing on your plate, you paint on it. I find the painted-on pentacles to be a bit more vibrant than the ones created with marker, and the paint also provides a bit of texture. If you're using more than one color of paint on your pentacle, add each color of paint separately.

After the paint on your plate dries, place it in the oven for thirty minutes at 350°F . This will make the painted-on design permanent and generally dishwasher-safe. Baking should also make it safe to eat off (sometimes our ritual cakes end up on our pentacle by accident), but be sure to check the label of whatever paint you're using just to make sure. If there are any symbols you want to add to the outside of your pentacle, repeat the same steps for them.

These two techniques can be combined as well. I know some Witches who go back over their painted pentacles with a Sharpie or two to add a bit more detail to their designs. You might also want the pentagram in your pentacle to be created with paint, and then the symbols around it to be drawn in marker. When you are done drawing and painting, be sure to bake your plate for thirty minutes at 350°F.

Beeswax Pentacle

My wife and I's favorite pentacle is one we made out of beeswax. Not only are beeswax pentacles easy to create on your own, but they also smell great! And unlike ink or paint, beeswax is completely natural. I rarely see beeswax pentacles today, but they are the most traditional type of pentacle for Witches.

In *Witchcraft Today*, Gerald Gardner writes: "Let the Pentacles be of wax that they may be melted or broken at once" (chap. 4). Instantly broken pentacles appealed to Gardner because he was writing at a time when practicing Witchcraft was still likely to cost a person their job or family, so being able to hide the tools of the art was of absolute importance. On a beeswax pentacle, the pentagram, along with any other desired symbols, are simply etched into the wax, and can be easily wiped away with your hand on a warm day.

To make your own beeswax pentacle, you'll need either a ceramic plate or a decorative metal one. My wife and I found a suitable metal plate at a local secondhand shop and paid less than a dollar for it. I think it was originally a plate used to commemorate a birthday or anniversary, and had bunches of grapes around its edges. (As followers of Dionysus, it was perfect for us!) Ceramic or metal both work well, but since metal plates are somewhat rare today, I think they add a unique touch to the beeswax pentacle.

Beeswax pentacle

After you've selected your plate, you'll need to acquire some beeswax. Beeswax is available at many natural food stores as well as some craft stores. We picked ours up at a local farmers' market. We found a booth selling votive beeswax candles and picked up two, which was more than enough wax for our small plate, which is about five inches across.

Once you've acquired your plate and beeswax (and removed the wick if necessary), place your plate on a baking sheet and set your oven to between 180° and 190°F (which is generally the lowest setting on an oven). Baking your beeswax at a low temperature will preserve the smell of your wax, and it's a welcome scent in ritual! To avoid any potential cleaning catastrophes, line your baking sheet with aluminum foil in case the wax flows over the edge of your plate. Place your beeswax on the center of your plate and then bake for about forty-five minutes. When you open your oven back up, the beeswax should be completely melted and will have pooled in the center of the plate. Remove the baking sheet with your pentacle on it from the oven, and allow to cool for a couple hours.

While my wife and I have never had any trouble melting beeswax for the creation of a pentacle, others have had much less luck. Ceremonial magician Lon Milo DuQuette once set fire to his house when melting beeswax escaped from the cookie sheet his pentacle was sitting on and dripped onto the floor of his oven (yikes!). It goes without saying that anytime you are using an oven, you should be sure to check in on things, and just in case, be sure to open the oven door a few times to make sure nothing is amiss.

After the wax has cooled, you are now ready to etch a pentagram onto your plate. If you want to create your pentagram in the most witchy way possible, you can use your white-handled knife or athame to carve your pentagram into the wax. Alternatively, you can also use a pin, an X-Acto knife, a box cutter, or a ballpoint pen. What's most important is to use whatever tool you find most comfortable.

If you use a metal plate, it can be difficult to add additional symbols around the edges of your pentacle. My wife and I overcame this problem by etching a rather small pentagram into the middle of our pentacle, leaving lots of space for other symbols. Another solution is to add whatever symbols you want between the five points of your pentagram.

While our pentacle was created with a metal plate, a ceramic plate provides some extra options. Using paint or a marker, you can place symbols on the raised part of your plate before adding the beeswax and etching the pentagram into the middle. If you go this route, you'll want to add the outside symbols first, bake your plate to make them permanent, and then melt your beeswax onto your plate.

A beeswax pentacle does require a bit more work than other homemade pentacles. Over time you'll have to re-etch your symbols back into the wax, and may even need to remelt the wax in order to do so. Since wax is sticky, it also has a nasty habit of picking up whatever dirt, dust, or cat hair is floating around the house. This can be cleaned up with a damp cloth, but after a few years you may find yourself having to replace the wax completely. Despite these drawbacks, I highly recommend beeswax pentacles.

ALTAR-NATIVES

Pantacle for the Impatient, Lazy, Inept, or Hopelessly Awkward Magician

IF WORKING WITH beeswax seems beyond your artistic skill level but you still want to create a bona-fide magick pantacle, you can do this:

1. Go to an arts and crafts or hobby store and buy a round wooden disk, such as those manufactured for plaques, photo mounting, etc.
2. Lightly sand, smooth, and brush clean the disk.
3. Take a photocopy of your design (carefully trimmed to fit handsomely to the wooden disk) and spray the back of the paper with spray adhesive (available at the craft store).
4. Carefully adhere the paper drawing to the wood, being careful to avoid bubbles.
5. Let dry overnight.

6. Using a clear commercial glossy or semi-glossy finisher, spray or brush-seal the disk, front and back, following the directions on the can. Ask for suggestions at the craft store where you bought your wooden disk.

Lon Milo DuQuette
Method from *Homemade Magick: The Musings & Mischief of a Do-It-Yourself Magus* **(Llewellyn, 2014).**

Pentacle Rituals

In most Witch ritual, the pentacle is generally used as an "altar on the altar." It's where the elements (water, incense, salt, and fire) are blessed and consecrated. Many covens also bless their cakes and ale upon it as well. In this section I've included some of the more common rites using the pentacle, along with a few extra ones. The pentacle is often overlooked in ritual, but it's a powerful tool with many uses.

Consecrating and Activating the Pentacle

Because the pentacle serves as a conduit for divine energy, it's important to properly consecrate and activate your pentacle in order to get the most out of it in your magickal endeavors. Most tools of the art don't require an activation ritual, but most tools aren't designed to transmit energy from one realm to the next! The pentacle is unique in this way, and that uniqueness requires a different sort of rite beyond the standard blessing and consecration.

Almost all ritual tools are blessed and consecrated, a function that serves a variety of purposes. Consecration dedicates an object to a particular use. In this case we'll be dedicating the pentacle to the Craft of the Wise and the magickal practices that are a part of that craft. When consecrating an item for individual use, consecration serves as a way of bonding that tool to its owner. Our tools should be extensions of ourselves, and consecration helps achieve that. Finally, I believe that consecration makes an item holy, as its use is often dedicated to the Goddess and God (or other deities and/or higher powers).

I do believe it's possible to activate a pentacle simply by using it and making it a vital part of the Witch's altar. However, such a process takes a long time. This ritual speeds up that process and will have your pentacle conjuring up the magick it's meant to summon forth a lot more quickly.

Before beginning your consecration ritual, make sure to have the four elements represented on your altar. I suggest using water (water), incense (air), salt (earth), and a lit candle (fire). It's also important to have something representing the Goddess and God. Deity statues are the standard here, but the Lord and Lady can be represented in more abstract ways as well. For instance, my wife and I often represent the

Goddess with a seashell and the God with a pine cone. What's most important here is that whatever you use makes sense to you.

Once your altar is properly prepared, start the ritual by setting up your sacred space in the usual way (casting the circle, calling the quarters, and invoking the Lord and Lady). Begin the consecration rite by stating your intentions to the universe:

> *Tonight I dedicate this pentacle into the service of the Lord and Lady to assist me in my journey as a Witch. May its power bless and charge my rites and lend the energies of the Old Ones to me and those I love in this life. So mote it be!*

Now pick up your pentacle and place it in the smoke of your altar's incense. Try to move your pentacle around so the smoke touches every inch of it. As the smoke touches the pentacle, imagine that smoke removing any negative energies from it. While the pentacle is in the incense, say:

> *With the power of air, I bless and consecrate this pentacle. Spirits of the east, spirits of clear will and knowledge, I ask that you hallow and sanctify this pentacle for my use in the Craft of the Wise and the ways of the Witch. May this tool*

serve me well in honoring the Lord and Lady. Powers of air, hear my petition and consecrate this pentacle. So mote it be!

I like to run my tools through a candle flame when consecrating them, but depending on what your pentacle is made of, that's not always the best course of action. If running your pentacle through flame is going to melt the wax upon it or leave a soot mark, simply make sure the heat of the candle touches your pentacle instead of touching it to the flame. As you hold your pentacle above the candle's flame, imagine the candle's heat burning away any impurities on your pentacle. As the candle shares its power, say:

With the power of fire, I bless and consecrate this pentacle. Spirits of the south, spirits of passion and desire, I ask that you hallow and sanctify this pentacle for my use in the Craft of the Wise and the ways of the Witch. May this tool serve me well in honoring the Lady and Lord. Powers of fire, hear my petition and consecrate this pentacle. So mote it be!

Set your pentacle upon the altar and cup some water in your non-dominant hand. With your free hand, begin sprinkling the water onto your pentacle. As the water splashes upon your pentacle, imagine it working like a cleansing spring rain, purifying your pentacle and preparing it for magickal use. As you sprinkle the water, say:

With the power of water, I bless and consecrate this pentacle.
Spirits of the west, spirits of death and initiation, I ask that
you hallow and sanctify this pentacle for my use in the Craft
of the Wise and the ways of the Witch. May this tool serve me
well in honoring the Lord and Lady. Powers of water, hear my
petition and consecrate this pentacle. So mote it be!

With your dominant hand, pick up a small handful of salt and slowly sprinkle it over your pentacle. As each grain hits your pentacle, imagine the salt absorbing any unwanted energies that might be on your pentacle due to its manufacture. As the salt slowly falls on the pentacle, ask for the blessings of earth:

With the power of earth, I bless and consecrate this pentacle.
Spirits of the north, spirits of hearth and home, I ask that you
hallow and sanctify this pentacle for my use in the Craft of the
Wise and the ways of the Witch. May this tool serve me well in
honoring the Lady and Lord. Powers of earth, hear my petition
and consecrate this pentacle. So mote it be!

Finally, ask for the blessings of the Lord and Lady upon your pentacle. Start by placing your Goddess statue (or representation) upon your pentacle. Imagine her around you, and feel her power in your circle and in your work. When you feel her near to you, ask for her blessings:

Great Lady, Gracious Goddess, Mistress of the Moon, I ask that you bless and consecrate this pentacle. Let your love pour forth upon it so that it might aid me in my work as a Witch and a priestess! May it serve to sanctify and charge my rites, lending your energy and that of all that is divine and true. Eternal Lady, hear this, my petition, and consecrate this pentacle. So mote it be!

Remove the statue of the Goddess from your pentacle and place that of the God upon it. Just as you did with the Goddess, wait to feel the Horned One near you and in the circle before proceeding. When you can feel his power and presence, ask for his blessings:

Great God, Lord of the Hunt, Sentinel of the Sun, I ask that you bless and consecrate this pentacle. May your wild energies touch and charge it so that it might aid me in my work as a Witch and a priestess! May it serve to sanctify and charge my rites, lending your energy and that of all that is divine and true. True Lord, hear this, my petition, and consecrate this pentacle. So mote it be!

Now that your pentacle is consecrated, you'll want to activate it so that energy will flow up and through it. Start by taking a good look at your pentacle and imagine it as being akin to a door, with energy existing just on the other side of it. The purpose of this part of the rite is to "open up" the pentacle, much like you might open a door to let in a cool breeze on a warm day.

This next part of the rite utilizes invoking pentagrams, which are drawn in the air or on objects when summoning powers and entities into a ritual space or, in this case, an object. While there are invoking pentagrams for each of the four elements, many Witches (including myself) use just one of those pentagrams in ritual: the invoking pentagram of earth. Since it's our intent that matters most, and not how we move our fingers, what we use to draw the pentagram is mostly a matter of personal preference.

Invoking pentagram of earth

Pick up your incense and fan the smoke over your pentacle, drawing an invoking pentagram onto it with the incense smoke. As you draw your pentagram, say:

With air I do charge this pentacle to open and pour forth the
energies of the Craft. Let magick come into this place to bless
my rites and power my Witchcraft. So mote it be!

Next you'll want to draw an invoking pentagram to charge your pentacle with the power of fire. Candles can be messy, so how you proceed here will depend upon your personal preferences. If your pentacle is made of beeswax and you have a beeswax candle available, you may want to drip the wax of the candle onto your pentacle. Alternatively, you can place a sheet of paper upon your pentacle and pour your candle's wax onto it while drawing an invoking pentagram. If you're worried about getting candle wax on your pentacle, you can also simply hold the candle flame-end up while drawing your pentagram.

Whatever method you choose for fire, imagine the pentagram upon your pentacle alive with energy and power as you follow its outline with your candle. When I activate a new pentacle, I often imagine this much like an eye slowly beginning to open. As you trace the invoking pentagram, say:

With fire I do charge this pentacle to open and pour forth the
energies of the Craft. Let magick come into this place to bless
my rites and power my Witchcraft. So mote it be!

Dip your dominant finger into your dish of water and begin drawing an invoking pentagram upon your pentacle with the water. Visualize your pentacle sparking and opening up to the energies of the universe. Charge your pentacle with the power of water as you run your finger across it:

With water I do charge this pentacle to open and pour forth the energies of the Craft. Let magick come into this place to bless my rites and power my Witchcraft. So mote it be!

To charge your pentacle with the power of earth, scoop up a bit of salt and slowly sprinkle it out in the shape of the invoking pentagram on your pentacle. As the grains of salt fall upon your pentacle, imagine the salt activating the energies that will flow through it. As you sprinkle your salt, say:

With earth I do charge this pentacle to open and pour forth the energies of the Craft. Let magick come into this place to bless my rites and power my Witchcraft. So mote it be!

Place your Goddess statue (or token) upon your pentacle, and in your mind's eye, see her looking back up at you through the pentacle. See her as the moon, the beauty of the green Earth, and the jewel of the oceans. Feel her power begin to flow out of the pentacle upward and toward you. Place both of your hands around your pentacle, and as you do so, see yourself pulling energy upward through the pentacle. Your hands should tingle a bit as you start to draw the magick up to you. As you activate the flow of energy, say:

O Gracious Goddess, open up to me the secret doorway that leads to your most infinite rapture. Charge this gateway so that my pentacle might exist between the world of mortals and that of the Old Ones. Let it be an entryway into the realm of spirit and a light to bless and power my magick. So mote it be!

After you've removed your Goddess statue from the pentacle, place your God statue (or token) upon it. Visualize the power of the God just on the other side of your pentacle's pentagram. See him as the shining sun, the leader of the Wild Hunt, and the soul of nature. Also imagine him as the Lord of Death and Resurrection, welcoming the souls of the dead to the Summerlands before sending them back out to be reborn in this world. Place both of your hands around the pentacle and begin to pull the energy of the Great God up through your pentacle while saying:

Horned One, Dread Lord of Shadows, open to me the portal that leads from this world to the land beyond the veil. Charge my pentacle so that it might be a pathway for our Mighty

Dead and those we have loved and lost in this lifetime. May my
pentacle allow my magick to be fueled by the mysteries of the
end and the wonder of beginnings. So mote it be!

Your pentacle should now be activated and ready for use. Before ending the rite, be sure to thank the Lord and Lady, along with all the elemental energies that you've summoned. The more you use your pentacle, the more powerful it will become!

Blessing a Pentacle for Coven Use

When I recently purchased a new pentacle to use in the rites of my coven, I decided that a general blessing and consecration ritual for it was not enough. It needed a little extra ritual to ensure that the various gods and ancestors of every coven member felt welcome. If you have a pentacle set aside for coven ritual, I recommend performing this rite so that the individual energies of each covener (along with the powers they are connected to) are a part of the coven's pentacle.

Start by setting up your ritual space as usual (circle/quarters/deity, etc.), followed by the cleansing and blessing ritual just described. When all of that is finished, present the pentacle to everyone in the coven and explain how you want their gods, ancestors, and Mighty Dead to be a part of the coven's rites going forward.

To accomplish that, the pentacle should be passed around to everyone in the circle (clockwise), with each covener getting a few minutes to reflect on the powers that are important to them. While they are holding the pentacle, they should be instructed to look into it with their mind's eye and visualize their gods and ancestors. When that link has been established, they should then "pull" energy up through the pentacle, attracting those powers to the surface of it.

In order to pull ancestors, Mighty Dead, and goddesses and gods up through the pentacle, everyone should be instructed to hold the pentacle by the edges and look down upon it. In their mind's eye, they should visualize the forces that are most important to them in their practice looking back at them through the pentacle. While engaged in the visualization, they should flex the muscles on their forearms while willing the powers they honor to flow up and through the pentacle.

As Witches, we don't command or control deities or spirits, but we can share our intentions with them. I imagine the "pulling energy" part of this rite as a way of lighting a cosmic candle, alerting our ancestors and gods that we want them with us. We are firing up a beacon to give them directions up through our pentacle and into our circles and rites.

Once everyone has had a few minutes with the pentacle, it should be held up above the head of whoever is leading the rite. That person should then instruct everyone in the coven to repeat the following with them:

> *Ancestors of bone, blood, and spirit, be welcome here. So mote it be!*
>
> *Mighty Dead, those Witches and Pagans who have taught, loved, and paved the way, be welcome here. So mote it be!*
>
> *Lords and Ladies, gods and goddesses, those we honor in this circle, be welcome here. So mote it be!*

The pentacle should then be set in the middle of the altar, with the High Priestess touching it with her wand while saying:

> *Through this portal, all who love, cherish, honor, and respect those of this coven are welcome in these, our rites. So mote it be!*

The coven pentacle will now act as a lodestone, helping to attract those powers and deities that are important to everyone in the coven.

Blessing the Elements

The pentacle is probably most closely associated with the consecrating and purifying rites that many Witches use to begin their rituals. In these rites the four elements of air, fire, water, and earth (represented by incense, a lit candle, water in a bowl or chalice, and salt) are cleansed and blessed, with the salt mixed with water and the incense lit by candle flame. The combined and activated elements are then taken around the ritual space to purify it, and are often used to cleanse the ritual's participants as well.

Most books that contain elemental purification rites mention the pentacle as being a part of the process, but they don't offer much of a reason for it. They simply instruct the Witch to "set the salt on the pentacle," never explaining *why* the salt should be placed on the pentacle. What we do during ritual as Witches should have meaning and purpose beyond following rote instructions, and how we prepare the elements for ritual and what it all means is an extraordinary thing worth thinking about.

In my coven we place the incense, candle, water, and salt on our pentacle to infuse those items with divine energy. By placing them on the pentacle we are saying that these items are to be made pure by the power of the Lord and Lady and the magick that we wield in circle as Witches. While the salt and water are on the pentacle, our ritual leaders place their athames (ritual knives) into them, charging those individual elements with their personal energies. (In our circle I tend to consecrate the water and my high priestess wife the salt, and when the two are mixed, our energies are then distributed into both substances.)

While we don't use our athames when consecrating the incense and flame, we do use a pillar candle dedicated to spirit on our altar to light them. For us, the spirit candle represents the power that created the universe and holds everything together. It's the original source, the prime mover, the beginning of all things, and when using that flame to light a candle and our incense, we are uniting that power with the energy that comes through our pentacle. Fire purifies the candle and the incense, while the pentacle and the power of spirit consecrate the both of them.

I've written this ritual for solitary Witches, but it can easily be done by two or four different people depending on how you want to divide things up. If you are doing ritual with a group, I recommend including at least two people in the active process of this rite. In the end, there's no right or wrong way to practice Witchcraft rites. What's most important is to do things in a way that makes sense for everyone involved.

I've always placed our elemental blessings at the beginning of ritual, immediately after invoking spirit. Since spirit plays an active role in this rite (its power is a part of our candle and incense), I've included that summoning in this ritual. That summoning also serves as a blessing over the start of the entire ritual, and for that reason this type of invocation is often called a "blessing prayer." I perform this prayer before calling the quarters or casting the circle. Once I'm focused on ritual, I begin the rite by calling to spirit:

> *Let the power of the All be in this place, the cosmic echo, the shaper of the universe, that which is changeless and eternal.*
>
> *May the power of the Lady, the Gracious Goddess who gave birth to this world, and the power of the Lord, the Horned Hunter who shines as the sun, be with us in this place.*
>
> *Let the elements be present as we prepare to walk between the worlds.*
>
> *United we are with all that has been and all that will be, blessed be this place, and this time, and they who are now with us.*

After the blessing prayer has been said, light the spirit candle, generally a large pillar candle in the center of your altar. Once that candle has been lit, place the bowl/chalice/cauldron of water upon the pentacle. As you place it on the pentacle, visualize energy coming up and into the water through your pentacle. Then place your athame (or wand) into the water and imagine your own energy now flowing through the water, cleansing and purifying it, making it truly blessed and ready for ritual. I usually visualize this as a blue-white light, and in my mind's eye I can see that energy zapping away any impurities in my water. When you are satisfied that the energies of your pentacle and yourself are running through the water, say:

In the names of the Lord and Lady, I cleanse and purify this water. May my power and the blessings of the gods remove from it all impurities and uncleanliness. So mote it be!

Take the water off the pentacle and set it aside, replacing it with the bowl of salt. Visualize the energy from your pentacle coming up through your dish of salt, charging it with energy. When you are satisfied that the dish of salt has begun to absorb the pentacle's power, place your athame into the bowl of salt. Push cleansing energy out of yourself and through the athame, willing it to cleanse the element of earth now on your pentacle. When your energies and those of the pentacle have both entered the salt, say:

In the names of the Lord and Lady, I cleanse and purify this salt. May my power and the blessings of the gods remove from it all impurities and uncleanliness. So mote it be!

Now that the salt has been blessed and consecrated, use your athame to place three blade-fuls of salt in the water. While doing this, say *Thrice measured! Thrice taken! Thrice given!* and mix the salt and water together with your blade. (In this instance, you have measured the salt three times, taken three measures of it, and then given those measures to the water—thus these words.)

Set the bowl of salt and the bowl of salted water aside and place your candle (and candleholder) representing fire upon the pentacle. Light a taper from the spirit candle and then use it to light your fire candle. As the wick begins to burn, say:

May the purifying power of the flame most sacred bless and consecrate this agent of fire. May the gods bless this light so that it will purify our rites. So mote it be!

After the candle is lit, blow out your taper. (Alternatively, you can just pick up your fire candle and light it directly from the spirit candle.)

Replace the candle with your incense, lighting the taper this time from your fire candle. When the incense begins to smoke, say:

Blessings be upon thee, instrument of air. With the purifying power of the flame most sacred, we consecrate thee. May your purifying smoke serve both us and the gods and prepare this space. So mote it be!

The salted water should now be sprinkled around the ritual space in a clockwise direction. Use it to cleanse the ritual's participants and the space itself, making sure to pay special attention to doorways, windows, and any corners that might have attracted some negative energies. The incense should be taken around the circle next, with the smoke being directed into corners and around those gathered at the ritual. With your energies, the power of spirit, and the blessings of the Lord and Lady radiating through the pentacle, your space and all participants should truly be ready for ritual.

CHAPTER FOUR

Building an Altar
(Tempest)

In this chapter we'll tackle everything you should consider when you decide you'd like to make an altar. First we'll talk about what you can use your altar for. Then we'll look at how important location and structure can be, and if size really does matter. We'll also consider what should and shouldn't go on the altar. Throughout this whole section, we'll see that careful planning can prevent problems further down the line—saving you time, money, and possibly your sanity.

First Things First

There are some important questions you need to consider before setting up an altar:

Are you setting up one general altar, or do you plan to have multiple altars for specific things?

One general altar is great, especially if you are limited on space. If you're thinking of having multiple ones besides a main working altar, here are some common variations:

- An altar dedicated to a certain deity or set of related deities
- A set of elemental altars, each one focused on a specific element and related spirits/deities
- An ancestral altar
- A personal altar versus a group/coven/family altar

What kinds of activities do you plan to use your altar for?

This will affect the location, size, height, and other important factors regarding your altar setup. Will you need a lot of room to move about, or will the altar move with you? Will smoke and flame be an issue? Do you need natural light or access to the outdoors?

Who else will interact with the altar?

Will it be just you? You and a partner? A small coven? A large group or congregation? Does your altar need to be hidden from view or otherwise private, or can it be viewable by family, roommates, neighbors, the general public, etc.?

What Do You Use an Altar For?

While the answer to this question might seem obvious, I think it's one that many people don't think that deeply about. An almost instinctual response to being on this path tends to be: "Okay, I'm going to be a Pagan/Wiccan/Witch. I need to have an altar!" So then you find a place in your home and put some ritual tools on it, along with a statue (or twelve) of deities, and light some candles when you need to do a spell, when it's an esbat or sabbat, or when you remember. If you don't know all of the possible ways that you can use an altar, it's easy to forget about it.

Devotion

Devotion is most commonly defined as religious worship or observance of some kind, typically focused on one or more deities. To be devoted means to be loving, loyal, or dedicated to someone or something. Acts of devotion at an altar could be saying prayers, chanting, singing, dancing, talking, and other exchanges of physically based energy. Other acts of devotion include maintaining the altar, cleaning and adorning statuary or other objects related to a god or gods, and making physical offerings in the form of food, drink, tokens, incense, smoke, etc. Often these elements are worked into ritual, spellcraft, and other activities, but they can also be the sole purpose for visiting the altar.

Working with deities does not automatically equate with worshiping them either. Some traditions actively embrace a relationship with their deities that they personally define as worshiping. Others may acknowledge the deities but consider their activities as a partnership. Both may have statues of deities on their altars, but how they see devotion and interact with the deities may differ drastically. I think a good way to describe the difference in practice is that in the former, the images of the gods on their altars is in recognition of their service, with a sense of exaltation and reverence. In the latter group, those images are like photos of their friends and family that they may place at their desk to remind and inspire them.

Ritual Focus

For many Witches, the altar is the focal point of activity for a ritual. It may be placed in the center of the space, in a particular corner, or on a certain edge. The altar's size and location in this format is fluid, its form and place determined by the needs and rules of the practice. For example, it could be on top of a table, on a rock or within a circle of rocks on the ground, in or around a cauldron, or on or around a stang, a marked space or design drawn in the ground, a sacred fire, the edge of an ocean or other body of water, a nest (human-made or abandoned animal-made), and so forth. The most important thing is that it works for whatever needs to be done before, during, and after the ritual. The altar is not just a decorative backdrop for the ritual, but is the place where any energy raised is directed toward/at. It serves as a functional location for objects of devotion to be placed and seen, the safe and handy home of ritual tools that are being used during the ritual, and the physical working site for certain tasks.

Consecration

Consecration means to make something holy. It is a process where you take an object outside the parameters of the normal or ordinary world and make it exclusively sacred and part of the divine realm. Tools that will be used solely in ritual are typically consecrated before they are actively used in sacred space (as we saw in the previous chapter). If it's something that is going to be used specifically in service to the deities, then it will be consecrated. An athame that is used only in a ritual context is consecrated, but a butter knife that goes back to the kitchen after you're done with it is not.

Offerings and Sacrifice

Alongside consecration, we have offerings and sacrifices. Items that are offered to deities, spirits, and ancestors for their exclusive use are technically consecrated but fall into a different category than tools and similar kinds of objects. If we give up something that is otherwise useful or meaningful to us, it becomes a sacrifice. Often this includes food and drink, but there are kinds of sacrifices and offerings that aren't so edible in nature—in particular those that involve our time and focus, such as prayer and meditation, or that make use of our bodies through song and dance. There is also the refraining from or giving up of an activity, such as fasting or abstaining from alcohol or sex.

Offerings and sacrifices have a multitude of applications as well. They can be used to fulfill part of a contract or an agreement with a deity or spirit, to build and strengthen a relationship, or to celebrate an occasion. They can also be offered in thanks, praise, or appreciation, or be a sign of welcome or hospitality or a request for cooperation, or be used for appeasement.

Blessing

Sometimes people confuse consecration with blessing. To bless is to bestow positive energies and/or divine favor on a person, place, or thing. It can also be an infusion of energies through exposure or by association. An easy way to remember the difference between the two is to think of "the blessing of the fleet." In many seaside towns where fishing has been a large part of their history and industry, boats are decorated and paraded out to be blessed by the clergy and the divine at certain times of the year. The boats are utilitarian—their tasks are not sacred—so they're not consecrated. Rather, the fisherfolk seek the blessings of the divine to ensure a good catch, request favorable conditions, and protect them from harm.

Some people bless objects simply by placing them on their altar for a certain amount of time. Other people place things there during certain events, such as a full or new moon, an eclipse, a special feast day, or a sabbat. Things can also be blessed when placed on an altar during a rite or ritual. Many people like to place jewelry on an altar to infuse it with power so they feel protected when they wear it. Others keep stones and crystals there to be cleansed and charged.

Magick and Spellcraft

Some Witches use their altar as a metaphysical workbench. It's the place where they may dress and light candles, mix together herbs, oils, and salts, make poppets, prepare satchets, and craft other concoctions and creations. Most often, all of the materials they need for spellcraft are stored close by and within reach—jars of herbs, vials of oils, minerals, salts, candles, ink, paper, ribbons, etc.—and the altar is centrally located. This doesn't mean that magick happens only at the altar, but it's often the starting point (if not the ending point as well) for a working. For example, a Witch may prepare all of the ingredients required for a house blessing at their altar. The water may be blessed at the altar, the fire for the herb bundle or incense ignited, and the deities and/or spirits called upon to aid in the spell, but then the actual act of blessing windows, doors, and spaces is carried out away from the altar. Similarly, a candle can be carved, anointed, dressed, and blessed at an altar, then gifted to a friend to use for their own working, perhaps on their altar.

Meditation

Sometimes the activity that takes place at an altar is far more low-key in appearance, such as meditation. Your altar can be a place that you stand, sit, or lie in front of, and then just allow yourself to become quiet. It can be a wonderful place at which to contemplate, focus, and find peace and resolution. You can use your altar to ground and center your mind and body, or it can be a place of departure for astral projection, vision flight, and other forms of spirit travel. You can also use meditation as a way to communicate with deities or spirits.

Divination

Many Witches perform divination at their altars—scrying, dowsing, laying out tarot or oracle cards, or throwing runes, shells, or bones, etc. Witches who do divination away from home, such as at shops, festivals, fairs, and other events, often bring a travel altar with them. If you look at divination as opening a window for looking into the past, present, or future, it makes perfect sense that you'd like to contain that energy and protect yourself by doing so in sacred space. If your form of divination is linked to working with specific spirits, especially through channeling and other forms of body-

Inspiration altar

based mediumship, then the altar is a gateway to that energy as well.

Honoring

Honoring is the act of remembering loved ones who have passed, ancestors, and the Mighty Dead at your altar. It may involve several elements of the activities already listed, but I feel it belongs in its own category. Devotion to deities is conceptually different than honoring the memory of the deceased. We recognize where we have come from through acknowledging our ancestors, but we also know that one day we will become ancestors for others as well. We're not worshiping the dead, we're remembering our ties to them.

Inspiration

As an artist and a designer, I find that many of my altars are centered around gathering inspiration. Some of them incorporate specific deities or spirits, and others are more of an homage to a specific kind of art, theme, or collection of pieces. This may not coordinate with other people's ideas of altars, but when your primary metaphysical practice is expressed through art, it is definitely fitting. The same could be true for someone who is a Kitchen Witch, gathering recipes and ingredients, or any other kind of maker who takes the physical and transforms it into the metaphysical.

Location, Location, Location!

As they say in real estate, location is everything. However, the ideal location is one of those things that is entirely dependent on each person's needs, wants, and limits. So how do you choose where to put your altar? Well, on one hand there is metaphysical and mythical lore to consider. On the other there is what makes the most sense for your practice and lifestyle (budget, schedule, privacy, and housing). Let's explore all of the possibilities.

Practical Matters

In order to set up an altar, you need to think about how you're going to use it. Is it something you are going to stand in front of for long periods of time? Then it should be at a height that is comfortable for you, with proper footing underneath, like a rubber work mat or a thick, cushy rug with a pad underneath it. Would it be better for you to sit or kneel to do what you need to do, like for meditation or trance work? Then you will want the altar to be at a height that works for those positions. Do you need it on a table, at a height where you can easily see and move things around with your hands? You can do bodily damage to yourself by working on a surface that is too low for you, so you definitely want to avoid that. If you need a lot of natural light, then placing it by or under a window will be best. If you have items that you need to plug in, or you have to use artificial light (beyond candles), then placement near an electrical outlet is an important consideration. If you plan to use fire in your cauldron or light candles, incense, etc., then make sure you don't put your altar too close to the smoke detector—or in front of a low-sloping ceiling that will easily catch soot and smoke stains.

Out of the Broom Closet, or Way in the Back?

Does your living situation require you to keep your practice private, or can you be open about it? If you own your own home or live in a situation where your beliefs and practices won't draw fire if they're out on display to whoever stops by, then generally how "public" your altar is tends to be of little concern. But unfortunately a lot of folks must exercise discretion because of their living situation and must be more private about their spirituality and workings. That requires some creativity and other forms of problem solving.

As someone who has rented (apartments and houses) since I was eighteen, I have been relatively lucky that my profession has not been an issue with the majority of landlords I've had. Not that I put "Witch" on my applications, but "Artist/Designer" has been there under employment—which has been viewed as a desirable occupation by most of the landlords I've had. (Artists generally have a reputation for beautifying and taking care of properties—at least the gainfully employed, stable-appearing kind.) Then again, my altars probably look like beautiful still-life displays or eclectic centerpieces to the untrained eye. Though once when I was moving to another state, I did have an over-eager real estate agent who wouldn't stop bugging me to show the house we were vacating, even though the landlord himself wasn't in a rush and was fine with waiting for us to move out. I finally agreed to a time, and have never seen someone go in and out of a house so fast. The landlord never called me again to try to schedule an appointment. It might have been the altars with deity statues all around the dining room or perhaps the ten-foot-long papyrus scroll from the Egyptian Book of the Dead on the wall that scared them off.

So let's say you need something a little more discreet, but you can take up some real estate to do it. Then placing your altar in a cabinet that has opaque doors that are easily opened is a great option to consider. When I lived in New England, armoires were generally easy to come across for not a lot of money, even antique ones. Any area where the houses were built without ample closet space tends to have a lot of armoires and similar-style dressers at the used furniture stores. More recently, a lot of contemporary furniture makers have been crafting entertainment systems where the television and other electronics are hidden when not in use. These too can make a great place for a hideaway altar. But you don't need a large piece of furniture for an altar. Smaller curio cabinets, decorative shelving units with doors, and bathroom medicine cabinets can all double as places for hidden altars and craft supplies.

Other creative solutions for keeping your altar out of view include roll-top desks, bread boxes, filing cabinets, coffee tables that have hidden drawers or removable tops, trunks, antique or vintage luggage, hat boxes, jewelry boxes, silverware chests, antique or DIY wooden crates, and other decorative boxes that you can find in the housewares section of most big-box stores. Don't be afraid to scour secondhand stores. You can score some amazing pieces there for not a lot of money. The same is true at salvage yards/shops, where builders deposit decent reusable fixtures, including cabinets, shelving, furniture, and more. I've bought heavy-duty loose wooden shelves to build shrines and special boxes for altars, and I often see a lot of bathroom cabinets there as well. Depending on size, these can sit on the floor or on top of a table, or be mounted to the wall.

If you're good at woodworking, you could build yourself a very special cabinet. You could design it to your exact space and specific needs, and install a lock if you so desire.

Shelf Solutions

Shelves may not seem as exciting as a beautiful table or cabinet, but sometimes the only space you can make work is wall space—and shelves come in really handy if you're on a budget. For under ten dollars you can secure a nice piece of wood or shelving and some brackets (IKEA has some pretty cool designs and natural pine boards), or you can check out what your local hardware or home improvement stores have.

I recommend going for a thick, solid shelf if you can, versus a cheap pressboard or chipboard shelf, especially if you have heavy statues or objects (crystals, cauldrons, cutlery) you want to put on it. This is even more important if you live in an area with high humidity, which will cause the shelf to warp easily. Otherwise you may find your entire altar in disarray all over the floor. You also want to check the overall quality of your walls. Most buildings made in the last hundred years have drywall, which is pretty easy to both install and find studs in (bonus points!). But once you go further back than that, you may encounter all sorts of plaster—especially horsehair plaster—as well as covered-over brick and other questionable building materials and methods. (If you live in New England, you can experience all of these in a single house.) If you're renting, make sure that installing shelves (even temporarily) doesn't violate your lease.

Wire shelving units can be extremely handy, as they don't need to be mounted to a wall to be secure and they break down fairly small when it's time to move. You can also set the height of the shelves pretty much anywhere you want, and store everything on them as well! But it sure can be difficult to set things on them that aren't large or bulky. So if you'd like to use a wire shelving unit to hold all of your magickal items plus an altar, I'd recommend getting a sturdy board that is a little smaller than the shelf you plan to use, and then lay it down. That way you won't drip wax or drop herbs and flowers, etc., in the openings in the shelves. You can also paint or drape fabric over the board to make it more visually appealing.

Which in a way brings us to another neat thing you can do with shelves. Whether you're using a shelving unit or a couple of individual shelves placed parallel to each other, you can make some very simple curtains with scrap fabric (or go all out to find the perfect fabric, if you have the budget) to cover your altar. This works if you need to hide your altar or you want to keep dust, pet hair, and other things from gathering on it. It also gives a neat "holy of holies" kind of feel to the setup. Depending on the type of shelves you have, you could use a spring tension curtain rod—the kind that twists so you can adjust the pressure so it "sticks" into place without nails or screws. Or you could secure a small curtain rod or wooden dowel to the bottom or front of your upper shelf, and then thread the fabric onto it, placing your altar on the lower shelf. If that's a bit too much work or investment of time/money for you, thumbtacks can do the trick!

Hidden altar shelf with curtains

Table Top

One of the most obvious location options for an altar is on a table. In the house I grew up in, the dining room table always had an arrangement my mother created that marked the changing of the seasons, but it usually was moved out of the way when we sat down for a meal. That's the thing about tables—we often use them for a variety of reasons: eating, working, congregating, gaming, etc. This makes it very hard to designate a table as an exclusive altar space if it's your main table, but it can certainly make a good temporary altar for special occasions. Smaller accent tables, on the other hand, can be used exclusively for altars. There's also a huge array of folding tables and trays that make it easy to create a temporary altar space for an event or ritual. They're easy to transport as well as tuck away when not in use. If you need your altar to be largely invisible, then using a folding table and tray when you do your workings is a great way to get the surface you need, when you need it, but also make it vanish when not in use.

Is Your Altar a Highway?

Another important thing to consider when setting up a permanent altar is how accessible it is to fur-babies and human offspring. Is it okay if your dog licks your cauldron full of water or your cat plays the testing-gravity game with items on it, or if small hands like to use your altar for playtime? If not, then think carefully about who and what your altar is accessible to, beyond yourself.

Cats and the Great Altar Highway

I have found that many cats do generally tend to be respectful of sacred spaces. I have watched cats carefully walk *around* spellcraft paintings that I laid on the floor to dry to get to their destination, and go out of their way to avoid walking on an altar. But I also have a cat who, as a kitten, took it upon himself to walk and jump on every surface possible, regardless of how high or seemingly inaccessible it was. It is because of him that all of my deity statues and other fragile items are kept securely behind glass in a curio case. They're still there, because even though he's not a kitten anymore, he's still trouble on four little white paws.

If your cat insists on making a home on your altar or playing with the items upon it, check out the cat-proofing suggestions in chapter 10. Although the easiest way to prevent young offspring, cats, and other creatures from messing up your altar is to keep it in a curio, cabinet, or other protected space that you can close the doors to and lock if you need to. You can also put an altar in a high location out of reach of small hands, but that may also make it out of reach for you—nor is it cat-proof, if you have a skilled jumper. If you insist on putting your altar out in the open, knowing that you can't always be there to supervise, then give some thought to what you place on it. What are you okay with getting broken, and what can easily be replaced? Can you keep implements in a locked box and just a few nonbreakable things out, with a pretty, washable cloth to define the space? If not, then resign yourself to your altar also being a highway and/or play station.

If you're dealing with human offspring (versus cats), one more option to consider is to give them their own altar. Many practitioners with children have told me that allowing them to have their own sacred space, just like their parent does, creates a lot of meaning for them. Considering that many childhood games and toys are designed to instruct and guide children in the ways of the world, having their own altar could certainly be a learning experience. They will learn to value their own space and treat it with respect—which could cut back on your own space being seen as a toy.

The Ready-Made Altar

You can also buy something specifically designed for an altar or shrine. Etsy is infested with overpriced premade altars—as well as some really beautiful furniture for ritual space. I've also seen some amazing pieces offered at metaphysical and occult shops, but that's not quite what I'm talking about. If you happen to live in an area that has a large Asian population (particularly those following a Hindu, Buddhist, or similar non-Christian/Islamic faith), you're going to find religious supplies in the local shops. Just like it's easy to find saint candles in most big grocery stores, Asian specialty shops typically stock incense, candles, and statues—and, if space allows, platforms, shrines, mini temples, and other kinds of structures for housing deities. As food, drink, and smoke offerings tend to be made regularly across these faiths, the structures are often extremely durable and easy to clean yet still very attractive.

Another favorite of mine are letterpress drawer trays. These are wooden trays with small separated areas that were used to keep printing blocks and type organized for letter-press and other kinds of printing. With the advent of computers and digital printing, most of them have gone by the wayside. But the trays can take on a second life, hanging on walls. They're perfect for housing small statues, ephemera, vials, stones, and other petite items, and they come in a variety of sizes, depending on the cabinet they came from. Type trays are most commonly found at antique and vintage shops, but they've gotten trendy in some areas, so now there are companies making replicas of them.

An Altar Beneath Your Feet

A little more rare nowadays is marking a floor to designate sacred space. From wood and concrete floors that have been painted on to elaborate tiling and carpets, I have seen some magnificent spaces where the floor marked out the quarters, elements, and other things important to that tradition or personal practice. If you like this idea but aren't able to alter your home's floors, consider using an area rug instead—either a plain rug that you can add things to, or heavy canvas that you can paint on and lay out easily without tripping on it.

Does Size Matter?

I think all of us dream of having a personal temple—or at least a whole room dedicated to just witchy things. But oftentimes economic factors present a challenge. With rising housing costs in cities, space is at a premium. Maybe you have room-mates or a similar kind of shared space, or small children. These are all important things to consider when creating an altar space.

Or maybe you have all the space you need but don't want to make something extravagant. No worries at all—because it's not the size that matters, it's how you use it. If you have a big, fancy temple room that you never use, that doesn't make you a better Witch. It may look really cool, but it doesn't score you any more points than someone who keeps their altar on a tiny shelf or in a small box. If you need or want to design a very small or portable altar, see chapter 9.

One last size consideration: is the altar suitable for the space you're working with as well as the number of people who may be working with you? If the size of your altar is too big or too small, you may run into technical difficulties during ritual.

A Room with an Altar View

A question I hear often is, what room is best to put an altar in? If you're living in a studio apartment, then your choices are fairly limited, often determined by the size and layout of the space. If you have more rooms, then it comes down to the level of privacy you require, the function of the altar, and the structure of your personal practice. If the only privacy you have is in your bedroom, then obviously the altar is going to be located there. If you're a Kitchen Witch, then your altar is probably best situated there, centered around the hearth or preparation area.

If everyone in the household respects, acknowledges, and plans to work with the altar, then a place where everyone gathers, such as a living room, family room, or den, is the best location. If you happen to have a fireplace, altars on the hearth are quite common and serve multiple purposes. If the majority of the work you do centers around working in or near your bathtub, then that is probably the best location for you. If having your altar in your bedroom affects your sleep patterns too much (this can happen with some sensitive people), then it's important to move it away from where you rest.

Align It with a Direction...Or Not?
(with Jason)

We've talked about many kinds of structures and room considerations, and now comes the next question: Where does the altar actually go? Some traditions have specific guidelines for where practitioners should erect an altar. Some say the east, while others say the north—each having an opinion about where a circle casting may start or end, and further connecting those directions with elements, deities, spirits, and/or ancestors. Being a practical Modern Traditional Witch above and below all else, I'm of the mind to say: put your altar where it makes sense for your space and practice. If you have a whole room or space that you devote to being a temple full time, then you can put an altar in every corner and facing every direction—plus another in the center if you so desire. (Yes, you can have *all* the altars!) However, I know that some folks may want more specifics regarding directions, especially from someone with a ceremonial background. So Jason has some excellent advice for you in the following section.

Placement of the Altar (Jason)

There are very few absolutes in Witchcraft, and this is especially true when it comes to the orientation of the altar. Oftentimes practicality will determine where our altar (or altars) sits, and sometimes we face our altars a certain way based on instinct or perhaps an inkling from the gods. Most working altars are set up in the middle of ritual space, but our altars and ritual actions often face a particular direction. Some Witchcraft traditions even mandate that the working ritual altar face a certain way, though these instructions are often unaccompanied by any reason why. What's most important in any situation is what works for the individual Witch, and this is most certainly true when it comes to an altar. However…

I do think there are compelling reasons to orient one's altars toward certain directions. In my eclectic coven, our altar faces east. I set it up that way because we begin all of our circle castings and quarter calling in that particular direction. It's our coven's natural starting point and it makes sense for us to orient our workings toward that direction.

The east is also the direction of the sunrise, which is a very traditional reason for setting up one's altar in that direction. The east is the direction of new beginnings, and every ritual can certainly symbolize a new beginning. The moon also rises in the east, which adds another layer to our altar's placement. The spirits of the east that many call to when summoning the elements are also often seen as forces of knowledge, clear will, and inspiration. Those three characteristics are essential for good ritual work.

I know very few Witches who orient their altars toward the south, but a southern-facing altar has some appeal. In traditions that honor a solar deity, it could be a way of showing that particular goddess or god respect. The energies of the south are also associated with properties such as lust and passion. A southern-facing altar at Beltane might help to pull in some of those energies, and might also be utilized in sex magick or any other operation that requires a large amount of passionate energy.

In my coven, the west is seen as a place of death and initiation, so an altar facing that direction might be especially appropriate at Samhain or any time we are trying to connect with those who have gone before us. Initiations are also symbolic of transformation, and the intent of ritual is to transform our mundane existence into something more magickal. Witches who feel a strong attachment to water might set their altar up in the west to tap into that power. (As someone who lives on the West Coast, this makes a lot of sense to me, and the element of water is traditionally associated with the west.)

The most common direction in which to position an altar is probably facing north, and most of the Wicca 101 books I've read have suggested as much. Because the north is seen as a steadying force, having an altar face the north is meant to give ritual a solid foundation. Writers such as Scott Cunningham suggest facing the altar toward the north because they see that direction as a place of power and as a way of connecting with the natural world.

How each Witch orients their altar is ultimately a personal decision, and there's no rule that says the altar direction can't be varied from time to time. If it feels right to you to have your altar face the west at Yule and then the south at the following full moon, that's completely fine. Experiment with what works best for you, and if one of the reasons I've outlined here for altar placement resonates with you, by all means feel free to do that too.

(Thanks, Jason!)

The Center Can Hold in a Circle

The location where you've placed your altar can either benefit or impede your practice. Even though I'm not ceremonially oriented with my Witchcraft, I'm also a professional performer, so I think a lot about staging. Whether it's dance, music, or ritual, I'm constantly evaluating the space in regard to surface, lighting, accessibility, drama, and flow. Sometimes placing an altar in the center of the circle (not aligned to any particular direction) can allow for maximum viewing of the working, and be best situated as a focus of energy. It can also make it fairly easy for a large group of people to move around. We also seem to respond well to gathering 'round the cauldron fire, whether it be real or symbolic in nature.

Why is staging important? Here are some things I've seen that have caused awkward issues during ritual:

- The altar being placed on an outer wall of a room, but the circle/working space is more central to the room, so the altar feels abandoned. Also, in this configuration, with a large enough group of people they will end up standing either in front of the altar with their backs to it or on either side of it—unable to join hands, if that's part of the ritual.

- The altar placed not quite in the center but not quite on the edge of the space, so people aren't sure whether they should go behind or in front of it.
- An altar placed in the center of the room, with the intention of it being accessible "in the round," but the altar is not laid out in such a way that it's easy to work on.
- Altars placed in the center of the room where there are plans to dance or do exchanges that require weaving throughout the room—and the altar placement does not allow for enough movement/flow around it without causing issues.

So it's wise to take into consideration the size of your space, the number of people you're going to be working with, how much time you'll have to explain how the ritual will work, and how important the altar is for your workings. If you want a central focus for your circle for everyone to gather around but don't have the space for something large—or access to a table—then think small and portable. A cauldron can always double as an altar, and there's a reason why stangs are popular in traditional Witchcraft (besides looking cool). They take up very little space, while being very visible and easy to decorate. If you're not tied down to a display of candles and ceremonial tools, then you don't need much stuff for your altar, do you?

Aids for Helping to Choose the Right Spot

We have talked about all of the practical and metaphysical things you should think about regarding the placement of your altar. What if you've got a few options and you're not entirely sure what is best? Here are some exercises you can do to help tap into the energy of your space and get some divine guidance.

Dowsing

Dowsing is commonly associated with using a divining rod to find ground water, but the word can also be used to describe the divinatory process for locating minerals, treasure, gravesites, and other hidden things. With dowsing, a Y-shaped rod or branch (each hand on a top part of the Y, with the end facing out or downward) is traditionally used to tap into energies or spirits that will direct the dowser to the location. Some folks may use their wand instead. The process is pretty simple. Just focus on the question "Where should I place my altar within my home/room/yard/etc.?" Then take a deep breath and clear your mind. If you feel a pull on your rod, follow it carefully to see where it leads you.

Pendulum

Another option is to use a pendulum. The pendulum is handy when you have a couple of places you are thinking of, but you can't decide which one. Determine what is a *yes* and a *no* answer for your pendulum, then go over to each of the places you are considering. Ask if this is the best place to put your altar, and record the results for each.

Tarot

If you're familiar with the tarot, you could also pull a card to see if a location will work for you. Of the minor arcana, I'd be inclined to see most of the aces and tens as a *yes*, as they mark beginnings and the completion of a cycle, respectively. If you have multiple location choices, you can pull a single card for each to see if that gives you a clear answer. Another option is to ask "Is this the best place for me to put my altar?" and pull four cards: three stacked to express where you are coming from, what's happening now, and what can happen in the future, respectively, and the fourth card signifying the overall result of choosing that location.

Meditation and Dreams

You can always do a short meditation before you fall asleep and then see where your dreams take you. If you have a hard time remembering your dreams, a waking meditation might be best. Sit in the room or space where you are thinking about putting your altar, cross-legged on the ground, if your body allows you. Close your eyes and focus your breath on your body, then visualize a taproot extending down from your tail-bone into the earth. From the center of your body, see a plant growing, expanding, and blossoming. In your mind's eye, focus on your altar and imagine your vines or branches reaching out to the place where your altar should be. Once you have identified the space, bring yourself back into your body and normal consciousness. Then get started!

What Goes on an Altar?

Some traditions are very specific about what should be on an altar, right down to the color and height of the candles and the size and placement of the tools. If you're reading this, there's probably a good chance that you're not from one of those traditions (otherwise you're just really curious about how the rest of us live). What goes on your altar is a matter of personal choice and the needs of your practice.

Basic and Beautiful

For an active working altar, I prefer to have things on it that double up in terms of form and function. I want the altar to be as visually stimulating as possible, but it's also important that the objects perform their tasks well. That means my candleholders need to be properly weighted so they're not easily knocked over, durable so they don't break if they do take an accidental tumble, designed to catch wax (versus spilling it everywhere), and easy to both light and extinguish. You might be surprised how many candleholders fail in most of these areas. The same goes for censers for burning incense and bowls for holding water and salt. We all love beautiful things, but something that's essentially a dust collector because it doesn't do its job properly can be a waste of space and money.

Ritual Tools

If it's safe to do so, the Witch's tools can live on your altar. If it's not a great idea to have a ritual blade or wand out in the open, then it's best to store it in a nice wooden box on your altar or close to it. Which tools you have and work with also depends so much on your path and practice. A classic Wiccan altar tends to have a cup or chalice, a wand, an athame, a bell, and an incense burner, as well as objects that represent the deities, sometimes represented as candles. Since ceremonial magic tends to utilize those tools often, it makes sense that those would be the ones found on a Wiccan altar. For those who don't work with ceremonial magic, their tools may be simpler and more utilitarian in nature: a mortar and pestle, a cauldron, and a candle. If you're unsure about what tools are right for you, luckily there's this really handy series of books on ritual tools...

So many statues

Statues and Divine Images

What represents the divine to you? Most folks find it very helpful to have statues, banners, or framed pictures of the deities and spirits they work with on their altar. I have to say, we're living in awesome times right now when it comes to statuary. When I first started on my path, there were very few choices in the ways of god and goddess statues, especially in an affordable price range. Now there are numerous artists and companies creating beautiful statues of nearly every pantheon you can think of, in durable yet affordable materials. Jason and I share an ~~addiction~~ appreciation for collecting them, though we haven't compared numbers. (It's not a competition...*yet*.)

There's also what I like to call deities in disguise out there in statuary. Every time there's been a Greco-Roman, Pre-Raphaelite, Art Deco, or Art Nouveau revival happening in modern culture, a new crop of classically inspired statues have popped up to satisfy interior-design tastes and garden fantasies. They may not have been intended to be items for worship and devotion, but they are often modeled after works of art that were! They also tend to be made of pretty inexpensive yet durable materials, such as poured concrete, cast ceramic, and plaster—though don't put the latter outside unless you want to see gods melt! If you find Demeter in a woman holding a shaft of wheat, La Sirène in a stately mermaid, or Pan in a playful satyr, there's no reason not to welcome them back into the fold!

You can also customize these disguised deities if you're handy with some paint and other craft supplies. If your deity requires a different skin tone (black, blue, red, gold, etc.), or needs horns added, or would look better with bunches of silk flowers or fruit glued on, then don't be afraid to alter and dress the statue as needed. In several traditions across the world (particularly some branches of Hinduism), statues are treated as repositories for the gods—so the statues are

Building an Altar

changed, updated, decorated, and refreshed to make them pleasing to the deity.

Or you could start totally from scratch! Ceramics, carving wood, casting plaster, paper-mache, polymer clay, fabric art, leather, metal, 3-D printing—the possibilities are endless if you've got the time, patience, and talent for it.

You don't have to go the statue route though. Depending on your space and budget, you can support community artists and craftsfolk who create art that you can hang. You don't have to go with original art either—most artists tend to produce prints and notecards of their work, which makes it very easy and affordable to both collect and frame. Or you can certainly draw or paint your own! If you're not so artistically inclined, you can also search for images of classic sculpture and paintings and print them out. If you really are inspired to take the time, you can create a collage or montage of images—focusing on either one deity or multiple ones.

Another creative option is to gather items that you associate with a particular deity or spirit. For example, a piece of antler may represent Cernunnos to you, or a peacock feather for Melek Taus, an arrow for Diana, a piece of amber for Freya, etc. Another subtle yet crafty option is to use jars, bottles, or small boxes as temporary vessels for gods or spirits—essentially making god houses or tabernacles. You can decorate the outside and put things that are special to those energies inside of them. What's especially wonderful about this option is that they'll be entirely unique, infused with your energy and intent, yet they are relatively simple to make.

Here is a welcome blessing for a new statue that you can use:

> *To (appropriate adjectives + deity's name + title):*
> *In your honor I place this image of you upon my altar.*
> *May your presence help me understand and cherish your gifts.*
> *May my workings invigorate and inspire your spirit in the world.*
> *And may our relationship be a blessing to us both.*
> *So mote it be!*

The Elements

Representations of the elements are commonly found on the altars of many Witches. For some, the elements are represented by the ritual tools through their associations. Others prefer to have more literal representations of the elements. Here are some suggestions of items you could use to represent the elements, although in the end it's up to you to choose what works best for your altar:

Earth: Items that can be used to represent earth include crystals, stones, bones, vials or small bowls of sand or earth, fresh flowers in vases, or potted plants. Silk flowers and artificial plants are good options as well, especially for those with allergies or busy schedules, or when the plants you wish to use aren't available in the current season or in your region, or perhaps your space lacks adequate natural lighting. I know that some people use fake flowers for budgetary reasons, but you don't have to think so fancy. There are many "weeds" that show up even in urban places that could be safely and freely wild-crafted for your altar: dandelions, grasses, clover, and so many more.

Air: Feathers are an easy go-to for representing air on your altar. However, be sure to research what feathers you can pick up off the ground or otherwise legally own. Chicken, peacock, pheasant, and ostrich feathers are often safe bets. It's best to secure feathers so they don't get blown off your altar or become cat toys. You could place them in a vase, tie them in a bundle with other objects, or pin or hang them up. Other ideas to represent air include clear or smokey crystals, flying insects (images, replicas, or preserved specimens), air plants, and wind chimes.

Fire: Unless you have the ability to safely burn a candle or lamp perpetually, most of the time your representation of fire will be something that has the potential to be burned or used for fire making or that came from a fire process. Matches, a lighter, flint, candles, oil lamps, lava rock, and coal are all possibilities. In terms of animals, reptiles are often associated with fire, so snake skins and vertebrae are options. Representations of snakes, lizards, salamanders, and dragons could also work for you.

Water: Water can be problematic as well, but in different ways than fire. Bowls of water left in the open can evaporate quickly, collect dust and dead bugs, become an attractive place for your resident animal companions to drink water, and cause staining, mold, and other problems if spilled and not cleaned up properly. That said, there are plenty of hassle-free ways to represent water on your altar. One is to have it stored in sealed bottles or vials. If you collect water from local sources, consider boiling it to cut down on microbes and such, then store it in a clean bottle. Other great options include fish scales or bones, shells, representations of water animals, and items from a pond, river, lake, or ocean. If you have the time, space, funds, and desire, you could incorporate an aquarium into your altar setup as well.

Still others do homage to the elemental spirits through images and statues of those beings. Here's a short list of beings considered to be elemental spirits—and there's definitely no lack of options when it comes to finding statues or artwork of any of these.

Elements on the altar

Earth elementals: Gnomes—plant and tree spirits, dryads, sprites, elven folk, satyrs, brownies, etc.

Water elementals: Undines—mermaids, sirens, kelpies, selkies, sea monsters, water sprites

Fire elementals: Salamanders—dragons and related mythical reptiles, creatures that breathe or emit fire

Air elementals: Sylphs—the fey (fairies), angels, and other winged creatures

Tools of Divination

I have a lot of tarot decks, but the deck I use the most lives on the altar when I'm not using it. The rest of the decks and divinatory items hang out on their own special shelves, organized like reference materials. Whether you actively work with cards, runes, bones, sticks, or a pendulum, most Witches find that keeping them on the altar is ideal. Not only is it a good place for them to be cleansed and charged, but you always know exactly where they are (as long as you remembered to put them back).

Backdrops and Backgrounds

To create atmosphere or for a more complete experience, you may also want to consider what is behind your altar. If there is a window behind your altar or the altar is in the middle of the room, then a backdrop really isn't that much of a concern. But if the altar is up against a wall, in a cabinet, on a shelf, etc., then you may find the space behind the altar to be just as important as the space you put the altar on. A backdrop helps to complete the visual experience of an altar. It keeps the energy focused on the space, helping to transport you or anyone else working with the altar.

There are a wide variety of backdrop options to consider. Behind your altar you can hang framed artwork, perhaps concerning the deities, ancestors, homelands, or your idea of "other space." Another easy option is to hang a tapestry or other kind of fabric, which you could change out seasonally or for other cycles if you so desire. Another very simple yet powerful option is to put a mirror behind your altar. If you work especially with other spaces/realms, personal reflection, and meditations, or you simply want to make the space look bigger, a mirror background is easy to acquire, and is relatively inexpensive as well.

Other Useful Items

There are some less ritually oriented tools that are good to have on or near your altar. They make your life easier and your altar less prone to messes and accidents. Here's a list of suggestions to consider, depending on your altar activities:

- Box of matches or a lighter (not accessible to small hands)

- Candle snuffer—Use when you have specific lore about extinguishing candles versus blowing them out. A snuffer also reduces wax mess.
- Hot plate trivet or tile—These are great for putting under cauldrons, censers, and other items that involve fire and heat.
- Trays for food and beverages—Whether you're leaving a food or drink offering or blessing food for ritual use, placing it on a dish or tray can help contain potential messes.
- Clean-up box—You may want to keep a small box or bucket of cleaning supplies nearby, including a dust rag and polish, an absorbent towel, baby wipes, and wax remover for physical mishaps. A spray bottle of cleansing mist/tincture is good for clearing out unwanted energies.
- Music—For many Witches, music is an important part of their practice. Having an MP3 player with a small speaker setup can take up very little space and be reasonably affordable—it doesn't have to be a fancy name brand to work well! You can create playlists of music for ritual, meditation, and other practices, and have them at your fingertips when you're ready to do some work.

Decorative Items

Then there are the things that can add another layer of beauty to your altar. I find that a lot of Witches tend to collect items that go on and off their altars for various occasions. I'm a big fan of exploring yard sales, thrift shops, and flea markets for interesting odds and ends that I clean and cleanse for my own use.

Altar cloths: If the surface of your altar isn't very inspiring or you want to protect it from wax, spills, and other accidents, you can cover your altar with a cloth. Fabric remnants can go a long way in sprucing up an altar space for not much money. You could have a variety of cloths for different seasons and sabbats. If you're especially good at sewing or embroidering, you could have a lot of fun creating altar cloths.

Vases: Having a variety of vases in different sizes can come in handy. Sometimes you just need a little bud vase for a single bloom, and other times a covenmate has brought a huge bouquet of flowers for the ritual and nothing to put them in. Look for vases that have a good, sturdy bottom and aren't prone to tipping over.

Dishes and bowls: I believe you can never have enough small bowls and plates for offerings. I also have a bit of a pottery fetish, so I'm always collecting little handmade pieces from other artists. Thrift shops often have loner plates for super cheap, and are a great way to collect interesting pieces to have on hand. That way you don't have to worry about Grandmom's dishes being accidentally broken, or where the twelfth plate of your wedding china has gone.

Candleholders: Holders are another thing that I have always found to be useful. I use tealights and votive candles, as well as small and large tapers for different occasions, so I'm always in need of something secure to put them in that's also aesthetically pleasing. If you're going to light a candle for each of the elements during a ritual, you'll need at least four holders to accommodate whatever size candles you are using, plus however many deity candles you may be lighting. I also collect lanterns to create ambient lighting in my ritual space (indoors and out). I cannot stress enough how important it is to put every kind of candle in a holder of some sort (outside of the seven-day candles that come in their own containers). Thinking "Oh, it's just a tealight in a little tin" or "I'm not burning it for that long" will probably lead to a mess. I will never forget a ritual done at the end of a Pagan leaders conference where someone bumped into one of the quarter altars and wax spilled all over the wooden floor of the rented space. The result was a bunch of us on the floor carefully scraping up wax—not the ideal way to end an evening. Actually that experience wasn't even that bad. I know of quite a few apartments and homes that have caught fire due to wax dripping onto fabric or a tealight without a holder lighting a table on fire.

It might be easier to ask what *doesn't* go on an altar. An altar isn't for storing random stuff, trash, or things that don't have a meaning/connection. Basically, things that don't belong on an altar shouldn't be there. But determining what stays and what goes has a lot to do with you and your relationship with certain objects. One person may feel that bones don't belong on an altar, while another feels strongly that they do—and both could probably argue with you all day long about why they feel that way.

ALTAR-NATIVES

Building My Altar

I STARTED MAKING my first altar in 1994, two years before my introduction to Paganism.

At the time I acquired all of the items I thought—well, actually I wasn't thinking at all. I was never into tchotchkes or knickknacks (just more things I'd have to dust), but there I was, mindlessly paying bottom dollar for a rag-tag, mismatched assortment of things that suddenly ALL MADE SENSE to me when I returned from England in 1996.

After being knocked unconscious by the Goddess at the Chalice Well, I returned home full of magick and wonder and earnest newbie energy, and I immediately thought, "Well, I'll need to set up an altar." I cleared off the mantel over my fireplace and thought of all of the items I would need to set up shop. And it was there that I received one of the biggest shocks of my life. After cleaning the mantel, I turned and looked around my living room, and everything I needed was already there.

I had apparently been unconsciously preparing for that moment for two years.

I've made a hundred altars since then, with other blades, cauldrons, rainbow flags, statues, Legos, toy cars, and whatever called to me in the moment.

My Goddess and God stand-ins always occupy the same positions on the yard-square table that has been my altar for eighteen years now: on the far, opposing corners. They are never together. (But now and then I do create lines of objects linking them together.)

I believe very strongly that one's altar should be a dynamic working area, one that is flexible and adaptive. My religion is one of reverence, yes, but also energy. If I neglect my altar, then I am also neglecting my gods and my religion.

I change my altar about four times a year on average. There is no set time, but I will eventually notice (often while dusting) that the energy there is old, and the theme laid out has passed.

So then it becomes *time*. Next to my table is an old dresser whose four big drawers are chock full of cloths and boxes and herbs and oils and statues and coins and shells and rocks and patens and mortars and pestles and cauldrons and cups and athames and hundreds of other items—the result of working in a witchy store for several years.

As I take apart the old altar, I dust and clean the items, and as I put them away, other items will leap out from the drawers and tell me they want to play. Once the old items are carefully tucked away, a new cloth goes on the table (Green? Blue? Black? What season is it? How do I feel? Where do I want to go?), the Goddess and God statues resume their stations, and then I figure out where everything else needs to go.

It's an exercise in intuition. Each altar is a schematic of my psyche, a board game, a rebus that explains where I am at on the Wheel of the Year and what I apparently wish to emphasize and accomplish during the next three-odd months.

I try to make the process as unconscious as possible. What I end up with is always striking and balanced and unique and strangely perfect.

I will often step back and think, "Ah, right. I guess this is what I need to do!"

My altar has seen me grow very much over the course of two decades, just as I have seen it morph and change with each new season. We are reflections of each other—and partners in time.

Angus McMahan
Angus McMahan is an all-around word jockey and award-winning storyteller. Visit him at angus-land.com.

The Coven Altar Cloth (Jason)

One of the biggest problems with building an altar for a coven is that most of the things on it tend to be owned by just a few people. The coven I'm a part of meets at my house, and the altar we use, along with most of the stuff on it, belong to Ari or me. During the course of writing this book, I started wondering if there was a way to create something that could be shared by our entire coven and be a part of our altar.

The answer to that hit me one evening while curled up in a t-shirt quilt on my couch. My wife and I's t-shirt quilt was created from a bunch of ragged t-shirts that represented almost two decades' worth of concerts, Pagan gatherings, and belly-dance camps. It's the one blanket in our house that was created (literally) out of our many adventures both in and out of Witchcraft, which makes it far more special than the rest of our blankets.

Something similar can be done for covens looking to add a bit of every member's energy to their altar, but instead of a quilt, we'll be making an altar cloth. I'm not particularly skillful with a needle and thread, so these instructions don't utilize that. This is a bare-bones, super-easy craft project that only requires an old t-shirt from every member of the coven, a table-cloth, fabric glue, a ruler, and a pair of scissors. Each t-shirt should be cut into a square panel highlighting the graphics and design on it. (If you went to a Loreena McKennitt concert, her picture is probably what you want on the panel.)

There are two ways to go about creating your all-coven altar cloth: precisely or chaotically. If you want a nice, evenly decorated altar cloth, you'll need to measure everything and then line up all of your t-shirt panels in a neat and symmetrical way. Alternatively, you can have everyone simply cut out their t-shirt panel in any shape they want and then glue it onto the altar cloth wherever they wish. I think the latter way of doing things makes it all the more personal, but I can understand people wanting everything neat and tidy.

If your coven has a lot of people who are good with a sewing machine, you can skip the glue and stitch everything together. But one of the advantages of glue is that the finished altar cloth will be much flatter, which will reduce the chance of a cup full of wine sloshing onto your pentacle. Fabric glue will hold reasonably well and stand up to the inevitable trips to the washing machine that most altar cloths make. Speaking of glue, when you create your altar cloth, make sure to distribute the glue as evenly as possible so it will have as few bumps as possible.

Once it dries, you're all done and you've got a very personalized altar cloth. Alternatively, you could have every coven member just write or draw on a tablecloth or create a personalized panel to glue onto it, but a t-shirt is often a little part of us. If it's from a well-loved festival or features a favorite band, it ends up with a little extra energy on it, which adds power to your altar, which adds power to your coven's rituals.

CHAPTER FIVE

Daily & Seasonal Altars
(Tempest & Jason)

Outside of daily practice and ritual, another way to deepen your practice is by adjusting your altar to reflect the changing of the seasons. This makes you consciously consider the weather, take note of the changes, and reflect on how this affects you physically, emotionally, and spiritually. It doesn't take a whole lot of planning or supplies to start a tradition or pattern in your life to help you connect more deeply with your path.

Marking Time (Tempest)

It may seem like common sense, but tracking the seasons has become a bit of a lost art. In our busy modern lives, far too often we find ourselves wondering where the month went, or did we miss a season? It's especially true if you work indoors most of the time in places that don't offer a lot of exposure to natural light. It's no wonder that so many people have seasonal affective disorder (SAD), when they're off to work before the sun has risen and get home after it's dark. There's also a psychological reason behind there being so many light-oriented festivities during the darkest time of the year, such as Diwali, Hanukkah, Kwanzaa, Yule, Advent, Saint Lucia, and so on. We need the light to illuminate our spirits. Like rabbits gone to ground for the season, we seek to burrow our way out of the darkness of winter to celebrate the return of spring. While many festivals are tied to religious events, often praising deities, the human element is crucial. These celebrations refresh our minds, bodies, and spirits, renewing our connection to the planet.

You may already do something special in your home to celebrate your favorite times of the year. It might be that you decorate the mantel above the hearth or the entry by the front door. You may have certain linens that you use at specific times, changing out curtains, bedspreads, and bathroom towels to mark the seasons. How and when did you start doing these activities? Is it something you learned from a parent or other relative? Were you inspired by a magazine, book, or friend's home? Is it something you do alone, or do you involve the whole household?

Items of the seasons

When it came time to write this part of the book, I kept thinking back to my mother, and how well decorated my parents' house has always been. So I asked her a few questions about how and why she does it.

Q. For as long as I can remember, you've always decorated the house for seasons and holidays. From wreaths on the front door and centerpieces on the kitchen/dining room tables to hearths and mantels, steps, and doorways—they all changed over the course of the year. You especially go all out for Easter and Christmas, but secular holidays and the turning of the year also get featured: fall, the Fourth of July, summer, etc. Did Grandmom do this as extensively too, or is it something you started expanding on when you married Dad? How much did having a good-size house and eventually three children influence it?

A. I basically started decorating the house for holidays when your brothers were little. I used to put up skeletons and Halloween things in the breezeway. Then I would do Christmas with lights, the tree, and wreaths on the doors, and even had a fake cardboard chimney in the family room before we had the fireplace. For Easter it was always bunnies and spring flowers and baskets of candy. I didn't do too much with a religious theme except to put up the crèche for Christmas and always an angel tree topper. I did put out a menorah as you guys got older [inherited from Tempest's father's Jewish side of the family]. As I became more interested in making my own wreaths, centerpieces, and crafts, I started decorating almost every holiday. We used to be a UPS drop-off/pick-up for Dad's music library, slides, etc. The UPS driver would comment on how attractive the breezeway always looked. I liked the look of change with the seasons, and it didn't cost too much, especially with me making most of the items.

Q. How does it make you feel to decorate the house? Do you feel obligated to do it? Why do you think you do it at all?

A. I've always wanted a clean house and one that looks nice. Since we couldn't afford too many new things, decorating helped spruce up the same old furniture. I probably started out decorating to amuse you children, but then it developed into something that I could personally put my stamp on besides the house being clean and tidy.

Q. Have you noticed any changes in how you decorate over the years? Have you added or subtracted any particular themes?

A. As you children got older and we moved, I turned to more seasonal decorations, like doing fall instead of Halloween, and a winter theme after Christmas, with just a touch of Valentine's and a bit of Saint Patrick's. Being at the shore, I go all out from Memorial Day to Labor Day with beach-theme accents plus Americana. I spend most of my time changing up the mantel. I like things coordinated. I don't make as many decorations as I used to. I find it hard to throw away old decorations, but I enjoy adding new touches.

———

So for my mom, decorating for the seasons is more about changing the feeling in the house, affecting and defining her space. The bunnies and the Christmas tree have much more

Daily & Seasonal Altars

to do with bringing the family together and recognizing the changing of the seasons than holding any specific religious significance. If my mom wasn't very religious this might not seem surprising, but she has been a CCD teacher and taught religion at a Catholic high school. She writes liturgies, designs masses, has been a Eucharistic minister, observes Lent, and goes to mass every week and on the special holy days. What my mom knows about Catholicism (and a number of other religions) would rival the knowledge of a fair number of pastors, ministers, and other clergy in the world. My mom's decorating the house doesn't make her a better (or worse) Catholic; it makes her a more complete person who is responding to her emotional, mental, and spiritual needs.

Until I interviewed my mom for this section, I didn't realize how much her habits and traditions have influenced me. I often hear Pagans talk about seasonally decorating their altars "for the gods," but I think my mom is more spot-on. We do it for us and our own well-being. I suppose if you want to look at it from a devotional standpoint, if we do things that help us enjoy life, then our joy and energy may please the deities and spirits we work with. But I feel it's important not to allow guilt to sink in if we can't always do something seasonal at our altars. We're not letting anyone down. But it does make for some pretty quick mental magick to do some sprucing up!

Now, I can imagine that some folks here may be thinking, "Oh gods, should I be changing out my altar eight times a year? I can't even remember when to get the oil changed in my car!" Or, "Where I live, there are only two or three seasons—if we're lucky!" I want to make it clear that you need to follow the seasonal schedule that you best respond to and that applies to you.

Personally, I am most inspired to seasonally decorate at the equinoxes: spring and fall, and Beltane and Samhain. I tend to bring out more lights around Yule to combat the darkness and a wreath of evergreens for the door, but I don't have any other typical holiday decorations anymore. But I do have special feast days and anniversaries that I observe through altar maintenance. So really it's up to you to decide when and how you wish to address the seasons and other changes through your altar. If you need some inspiration though, Jason has some fantastic ideas to get the juices flowing.

Seasonal Altars (Jason)

Many of us keep seasonal altars and are completely unaware of it. If you decorate your living room to reflect the turn of the wheel, you've probably got a seasonal altar in there somewhere. Seasonal altars don't have to be flashy, and most of my non-witchy friends don't look twice when we place Demeter prominently in our house every September. Even they know her myths!

Often the first altars we experience in our homes are fireplace mantels and bookshelves decked out in seasonal finery. When I was a boy (and still a Christian), I used to walk past the fireplace mantel at our house around Christmastime and wave at Jesus and Santa, who I just assumed were living there. They were the gods of Christmas after all, and that mantel held our stockings and several family heirlooms. To me it was something more than mere decoration, and I think most of my family felt that way too.

Today my seasonal altars are a bit more thought-out and contain more Pagan elements than the elaborate displays my grandmother set up when I was a child. But much of the intent is the same, and the seasonal altars in my living room today are a focal point for my wife and I's daily practice. We utilize them for small rituals and as a space to honor the gods we associate with each turn of the wheel.

I'd like to tell you that I decorate my seasonal altars uniquely for all eight sabbats, but that's not quite the case. I refresh them about six times a year, and the seasonal altars at my house generally run through the following cycle:

Autumn: My autumn altar is up from about the middle of
August through the start of October. Some of my autumn

decorations are removed for Samhain-specific stuff and then replaced in early November, where they stay up until nearly the end of the month.

Samhain: At my house, Samhain and Halloween exist side by side, with many of the things on my Samhain altar looking like they were purchased or created just for Halloween. I put the Samhain-specific stuff up in October and leave it there through the first week of November.

Yule: Growing up I absolutely loved Christmas, and as a Pagan I was delighted to find that most of the stuff Christians use to decorate originally belonged to us! Late November through the first week of January is generally reserved for Yule decorations, and when my non-Pagan friends come over they tell me it looks like Christmas has thrown up all over my house.

Winter: Quieter winter decorations go up in January and are generally subdued. They stay up until the middle of March.

Spring: By the spring equinox my altars are ready for spring and remain mostly unchanged until the end of May or early June.

Summer: The end of May is the traditional start of summer in the United States, and my summer altars remain in place until about the middle of August, and then the cycle repeats itself again.

I love decorating my seasonal altars with things that represent what's happening in the world just outside my door. As a result, my seasonal altars are heavy on foliage, fruit, and flowers. Some of what I use to decorate is natural, and some of it is plastic and is used year after year. Decorative flowers are especially useful because they never rot, and when Evie or Summer (our cats) tips one over, I don't end up with water all over the floor. I like using natural things when I can, but I don't think it's always necessary.

All of my seasonal altars have deities on them. Oftentimes they feature specific goddesses and gods, but not always. There are lots of deity statues available today, and many of them feature composite horned gods and goddesses, or represent the Lord and Lady of Wicca in various stages of development. When choosing a deity for a seasonal altar, what's important is that your choice makes sense to you. I offer some suggestions in this chapter, but we all have our own preferences, and the gods interact with everyone differently.

Witchcraft does not require anyone to forsake or disown their past beliefs, so if something was sacred to you as a child (especially around holiday time), there's nothing wrong with putting it on your altar. My grandparents gave me a miniature nativity set when I was in college, and it goes up next to all of our Yule stuff every year. Altars should hold the things, and sometimes memories, we hold dear. I find anything that links me to family sacred.

Because the seasonal altars in my house are set up proudly in our living room (one on a chest-high bookshelf and the other on a fireplace mantel), we also use them to add seasonal scents to our house. Because we find it less messy, we generally use candles scented with essential oil, or diffusers designed for essential oils. If you choose to add a seasonal scent, incense is another option here too, of course.

What follows are a few decoration ideas that I generally use at my home. As always, you should do what resonates most with you and your deities.

Autumn Altar

The fall is probably my favorite time to decorate, and there are so many options. My favorites are generally traditional: pumpkins (especially those mini pumpkins they sell now), sunflowers, and anything else related to the harvest. We like our house to smell earthy and inviting in the autumn, so tree scents and cinnamon are some of our favorite smells this time of year. Gods of the harvest and death are featured prominently.

Foliage: Leaves, pine cones, acorns, pumpkins, decorative gourds, sunflowers, wheat, dried flowers

Scents: Cedarwood, cinnamon, ginger, rosemary

Deities: Demeter, Cernunnos, Rosmerta, Dionysus, Ariadne, Herne

Other decorations: Bottles of wine, beer, or cider. Anything harvest-related, including cornucopias and tools such as the boline. I also decorate with deer antlers.

Winter Altar

Post-holiday season, I try to keep my seasonal altars sparse and tidy. Winter is not a time for abundance, and my altars tend to reflect that. I like decorating with driftwood or bare branches, along with lots of light to help drive away some of the seasonal depression. Gods of the returning light, which I tend to feel more at Imbolc than at Yule, make their home on our seasonal altars along with the Celtic Brigit. Due to Valentine's Day, roses feature prominently on our altars too. I associate winter post-Yule with "clean" scents like tea tree oil and ylang-ylang.

Foliage: Roses, bare branches, driftwood, cherry blossoms

Scents: Rose, ylang-ylang, tea tree, eucalyptus

Deities: Brigit, Apollo, Osiris, Skadi, Cupid

Other decorations: Lots of lights and candles to drive that darkness away and celebrate its return at Imbolc

Spring Altar

After fall, spring is the easiest season to create an altar for. Most traditional Easter decorations have at least a sliver of Paganism at their core, and all are representative of the Earth's returning fertility, so eggs, bunnies, and sometimes even Easter baskets feature prominently. A whole host of beautiful flowers bloom in the spring, and I try to keep them all well represented on our altar. With the return of spring also comes the return of Persephone, and I think it's the favorite season of the Greek Pan too! By May, jasmine is in full bloom around our neighborhood, and the scent is so strong that sometimes we don't even have to break out the oil.

Foliage: Tulips, orchids, hyacinth, crocus, witch hazel, early fruits

Scents: Flower scents, jasmine, lavender, neroli

Deities: Persephone, Pan, Tammuz, Eostre, Horus, Isis, Freyja, Freyr

Other decorations: Anything representative of fertility, such as eggs and rabbits

Daily & Seasonal Altars

Summer Altar

Summer might be the most difficult season to decorate for. The colorful riot of spring has moved on, but there are still several late-blooming flowers worth placing on the altar. We also decorate with grapes and grapevines, since the grape harvest begins in our area in late July. Perhaps due to childhood trips to the beach, I also like decorating with seashells, which are sacred to the goddess Aphrodite, one of our favorite summertime deities. Citrus scents are welcome, and in our backyard our lemon tree usually runneth over by July.

Foliage: Cattails, impatiens, summer fruits, daisies, marigolds, grapevines, grapes, ferns

Scents: Geranium, grapefruit, lemon, lemongrass, yarrow

Deities: Lugh, Thor, Sól, Dea Matrona, Belisama, Aphrodite, Gaia

Other decorations: Seashells, jars of sand or colorful rocks. Near the Fourth of July, I sometimes add some patriotic elements to my summer altar.

Samhain Altar

My seasonal altars for Samhain look much like the ones designed specifically for autumn but often are a touch more somber. Pictures of lost relatives get added to the seasonal altars when the veil is thin, and heavy, traditional scents from

Samhain rituals past, such as frankincense and sandalwood, fill the house. The deities shift too. Demeter leaves her traditional autumn spot to be replaced by goddesses specifically associated with Witchcraft, such as Diana, Aradia, and Hekate. And I often move Santa Muerte away from her private altar in my office to the seasonal altars to preside over our Samhain activities and to honor the Mexican Day of the Dead.

Foliage: Pumpkins, fall leaves, apples, pears, dried flowers, hay

Scents: Frankincense, sandalwood

Deities: Hekate, Aradia, Santa Muerte, Hades, Cernunnos, the Morrigan, Hel

Other decorations: Skeletons, jack-o'-lanterns, fairytale Witches, scarecrows, pictures of beloved ancestors and Mighty Dead set in prominent places

Yule Altar

Our seasonal altars at Yule are often mistaken for Christmas decorations, but the witchy associations are most certainly still there, as long as one knows where to look. Christmas deities such as Befana (the Italian Christmas Witch) and Santa Claus feature prominently, but so does Bacchus, whose merriment and mirth seems to be everywhere over the holiday season. Yuletide has long been a time for tricksters and figures such as the Lord of Misrule, which is one of the reasons Loki also makes an appearance in December. The house tends to smell like our Yule tree, making scented oil mostly unnecessary. And don't forget the Yule tree. For many children at this time of year, it is *the* seasonal altar, especially once the presents go under it.

Dionysus upon the Yuletide altar

Foliage: Fir tree branches, pine cones, holly, ivy, mistletoe, poinsettia

Scents: Pine, bayberry, peppermint

Deities: Sol Invictus, Bacchus, Dionysus, Loki, the Cailleach, Odin, Santa Claus, Befana

Other decorations: Stars, sleighs, fake snow, nutcrackers, stockings, and candy canes. Since most Christmas decorations have Pagan origins, most of those are fair game!

Building a Yule Log for the Altar (Jason)

One of the most cherished Yule altar accessories at our house is a Yule log. Unlike traditional Yule logs, this one doesn't go into the fire; it holds fire—in this case tealight candles! Our Yule log has space for three candles: one for the Goddess, one for the God, and a third for spirit and/or the spirit of the holiday. (During Yule rituals we've been known to invite the Lord and Lady, along with a certain visitor from the North Pole.)

A homemade reusable Yule log doesn't require much in the way of tools—just a power drill with a wide drill bit (bits designed for putting in doorknobs work surprisingly well) and either a saw or a hammer and nails, depending on how creative you want to get. You'll also need a log. This can be either something recovered from a walk in the woods or a perfectly shaped piece of firewood. To decorate your Yule log you'll need some craft glue and some pine cones, holly, ivy, bows, ribbon, or whatever else you want to use.

Start by making sure the bottom of your Yule log is flat and doesn't wobble. The easiest way to do this is to cut your piece of wood in half, but to do this evenly nearly always requires a band saw. If you don't have one, you can simply take a flat piece of wood about the size of your log and nail the two together. To make sure your base is festive, be sure to paint it green or red first!

Once your Yule log no longer wobbles, drill three holes for your tealights. Alternatively, you can use a smaller bit and drill holes for pillar candles, if you'd prefer those. The holes in the log should be an equal distance apart, which can easily be marked out with a pencil. Finish your Yule log by gluing whatever decorations you want onto it. The bottom of our log has pine cones, festival bows, and bells. The top of the log also has some shiny metallic ribbon, though it's kept far away from where the candles go. Once the log is decorated, light the candles and enjoy! This type of log is simple and beautiful and makes a great addition to any Yule altar.

Create a Daily Altar Ritual (Tempest)

Seasonal altars help transform both a space and our state of mind in a big way, but often don't require our attention every day. Usually we just set them up when the weather or calendar tells us to, and they stay fairly static until the next big change happens. Daily altars, on the other hand, require a more consistent, routine focus. Interacting with one's altar on a regular basis is a goal I hear most Witches and Pagans say they'd like to strive for. Let's look at some ways you can take on this challenge.

It's one thing to say you're going to start doing something every day, but it's another to actually do it. The reason for this is because we as human beings need to be stimulated or otherwise positively affected by our rituals. We need to feel that what we're doing is a valuable investment of our time and energy. We also have to be able to adjust our schedules to incorporate whatever we're doing without adding any additional stress. Lastly, we are more likely to abandon a pattern if we feel guilty about missing it, setting off a chain reaction of neglect and avoidance. That someone else (such as the gods, spirits, ancestors) will be angry with us—another indication of baggage. Our ancestors have been there—they know what living is like. The deities and spirits are rarely so caught up in our affairs that they are keeping tabs on us like attendance sheets. They may send or give reminders if you have made a promise to do a thing and fail to follow through, but in the end it comes down to you. The important thing to remember is that utilizing your altar is for your own benefit above all else.

So that begs the question, what do you *need* in your life? Do you have a time when you stop and consider the day ahead or process what happened during the current one? Do you need

Morning beverage and divination practice

something to calm you or invigorate you? Is there a meditation that you would like to start doing to help you achieve a goal? What about timing and your schedule? Would it help you to focus on something first thing in the morning? Would doing something right before you go to bed help you rest? Is there another activity you already do that you can connect to working with your altar?

Here are some ideas for activities to incorporate into your daily practice that hopefully you will find inspiring. This list is by no means complete, and it's really limited only by your imagination. You probably will find the greatest amount of success by linking your altar activities with something you are already doing—or find that you need to bring into your life.

Morning Beverage Blessing

Chances are that in the morning you start your day with some sort of beverage. If you make your coffee, tea, cocoa, or smoothie at home, why not include the enjoyment of that beverage in your daily altar practice?

Gratitude Acknowledgment

While this may seem like a trendy thing, it's been a part of my daily practice for years. At the end of every day, in my head I acknowledge and thank the deities, spirits, and ancestors that are in my life. Once I have done that, I identify a goal or desire I may have—it could be for me or a petition for someone I care about. If keeping it in your head doesn't feel right, you can say it out loud and, as you do so, light a candle or some incense, apply an essential oil to yourself, or water a plant that's on your altar.

Daily Divination

Doing daily divination at an altar is probably one of the most successful methods for a lot of people. If you're just learning a particular form of divination, it comes with the added bonus of giving you a quick way to practice. You don't have to look at a specific issue, but instead simply pull one card, stone, shell, etc., per day. Read into the meaning for that sign and make a quick note of it in a journal. (Writing things down helps you remember it better.) At the end of the day, you can compare how the day went with the reading of your oracle. I recommend working with your oracle in the morning instead of the evening, mainly because I know a lot of folks who can get too easily fixated on what they pull—and then you have to sleep on it! Pulling a card, stone, etc., in the morning gives you a few minutes to consider it and then go about your day.

Communing with Gods and Spirits

If the primary focus of your altar is working with deities, then it's probably a good idea to build up a daily practice to address that. For some people, that's taking a few moments to meditate quietly at the altar. For others, it's offering a chant, song, or poem for the gods, or just talking with them. Another option is taking the time to care for the deity statue or image—making sure it's dust-free, cleaning off old offerings, adding new decoration, putting fresh flowers in a vase for them, or giving an offering of food and/or beverage.

Movement Meditation

Do you do yoga, dance, pilates, a martial art, or some other physical practice every day or on a weekly basis? Do you do this in the same room as your altar? You can connect this practice to your altar, making it an offering, if that works for you, or a dedication to yourself or your health. Before you start, activate your altar by lighting a candle for energy upon it or blessing the water you will use to rehydrate yourself.

The Power of Practice

Perhaps your regular form of practice involves playing an instrument or working some other kind of art form. Before you begin your regular session, light a candle or make an offering at the altar to call upon a deity whose area of expertise gels with what you're working on. For example, consider Saraswati for music or Hephaestus for metalworking—or Brigid if you happen to be covering both. That way you may receive extra guidance and insight into your craft.

Medication Metaphysics

If you have a medication (or vitamins) that you need to take every day, tie this in with visiting your altar. If it's taken by mouth, bless the water and add the focused intent of the benefits of what you're taking. Often we get into the habit of tossing back medications without thinking about what their purpose is or why we take them. Taking a moment to think about it, and the results you expect, can add another layer of awareness to your physical and mental bodies.

Scheduled Routine Maintenance

Unless your home is a construction zone or it's pollen season or you don't do offerings of food, flowers, or drink, cleaning the altar every single day may be unnecessary. But you could choose to do it on a weekly basis, or even a monthly basis in alignment with the lunar phases. I find that the new moon is a good time for reflection and preparation for the next cycle. It feels good to dust, put things back in order, and contemplate what's coming up for me in terms of my practice, my life, and the seasons.

An Altar Dedication and Blessing Ritual (Jason)

Most Witchcraft books contain rituals for consecrating and blessing tools such as the athame or wand, but very few provide any information on dedicating an altar. Since the altar is often the focal point of ritual, it makes sense that it should be properly prepared into the service of Witchcraft. This rite blesses the altar and then welcomes the tools and materials that it will be home to.

Instead of using the standard four elements to bless and cleanse the altar, this rite utilizes essential oils. The ones suggested here all come from the correspondences found in *The Complete Book of Incense, Oils, & Brews* by Scott Cunningham (Llewellyn, 1989), but as always, the most important oils to use are the ones that resonate with you. I use this rite on my wooden altars in particular, because the wood will absorb those oils, giving them a sort of permanence in my altar.

Extra materials needed for this rite: Jasmine, rose, sandalwood, and cedarwood essential oils

Word of caution: Pure essential oils will often irritate the skin, so you may want to dilute the oils for this rite before using them, if they aren't already. (Because of the high price of rose, jasmine, and sandalwood oils, they often come pre-diluted.) Many Witches swear by jojoba oil, though standard olive oil will work just fine. For pure essential oils, add seven or eight drops of essential oil to $1/8$ cup of your base oil and then swirl the two together.

Before casting the circle and readying your ritual, you'll want to prepare your altar in the most mundane of ways by cleaning, dusting, and polishing it. Since none of those things sound all that magickal to me in the traditional sense, I prefer to do them before ritual. However, while mundanely preparing your altar, it is advisable to visualize the magickal work you'll be doing on it and with it in the days, weeks, and even years to come. That energy will enter your altar while you are cleaning it. The more you touch any tool and add your intent with that touch, the better your tools will perform for you.

Once your altar is physically prepared, proceed with your ritual as usual (cast the circle, call the quarters, etc.). For this rite I prefer to keep my altar entirely free of tools and statuary until those things are added at the end. If that's not possible, just try to remove as much as you can from your altar before beginning this particular rite.

Start by grasping your altar by its sides and pushing some of your energy into it. If you've never worked with the body's natural energy before, there are two easy ways to do this. The first is by flexing your biceps and clenching your fingers while holding on to the altar. When you release the tense muscles, you'll feel energy flow from them and into your altar. Alternatively, you can focus on the energy of the natural world and imagine that energy flowing into you with each deep breath. As you release your breath, pour that energy out of yourself and into the altar.

When you are confident that your altar has absorbed a bit of your energy, take the jasmine oil and place a small drop on the index finger of your dominant hand. In the center of your altar, draw a large invoking pentagram while visualizing that pentagram opening up your altar to the power and energy of the divine forces you will invoke during ritual. While drawing the pentagram, say:

By the power of the pentagram, I protect and consecrate this altar. Open up to me the doorway to spirit so that I may walk between the worlds. By the love of the Lord and Lady, so mote it be!

The invoking pentagram draws divine power into ritual space, and the jasmine oil is representative of air, since its scent so easily floats upon the breeze.

Place a drop of rose oil on your index finger, and picture the ankh in your mind's eye. The ankh has long been a symbol of life, and for many of us the altar is the focal point of our spiritual lives. Rose oil symbolizes love and passion, making it representative of the element of fire. Draw the ankh upon your altar, starting at the bottom and working your way up to create the loop and then back down to draw its outstretched "arms." As you draw the ankh, imagine your will being enacted during your magickal doings while utilizing the altar. As you visualize this, say:

By the power of the ankh, I call upon the life force to bless and consecrate this altar. May this altar serve as an instrument of my true will and fill my life with a passion for the path I walk. By the love of the Lord and Lady, so mote it be!

Ankh

Spirals have been used in religious worship for thousands of years and often symbolize rebirth. During this ritual, an ordinary table or bookshelf is turned into an instrument of the gods. If that's not rebirth, I'm not sure what is! Many Witches look at water as the element of death and initiation, and what is death if not a rebirth into another stage of existence? Sandalwood oil has a multitude of uses but is often associated with spirituality, which the altar is the ultimate expression of.

Place a drop of the sandalwood oil on your finger and begin tracing a spiral on your altar. The spirals I draw are always clockwise in direction and move inward toward the spiral's center. As you trace the spiral, see your altar as the center of your practice, and reserved now for spiritual purposes only. Verbalize your intent here by saying:

By the power of the spiral, what was once here has been reborn as the Witch's altar. This altar shall be a place of truth and beauty and an instrument of the gods and powers I serve here. By the love of the Lord and Lady, so mote it be!

The last symbol you'll draw with the essential oil is that of the eight-spoked wheel, which represents the turn of the seasons and the natural world. I've chosen cedarwood oil here because its smell connects us to the forces found in the natural world. When you draw your circle upon the altar, go clockwise, and then add the line cutting the circle in half where you began your circle. The remaining three lines dividing the circle into its eight pie pieces should all be drawn from left to right. While drawing your circle, invoke the power of the turn of the wheel upon your altar while visualizing how your altar will reflect the changing seasons:

By the power of the Wheel of the Year and the turning seasons, I dedicate and bless this altar. May it serve to connect me with the natural world and the yearly cycles of death and rebirth.

Here I shall celebrate the sabbats and the powers of Witch-craft. So mote it be!

The last half of the ritual is about welcoming all of your "Witch stuff" to your altar. Since altars serve a variety of purposes and can be arranged in all sorts of ways, feel free to pick and choose only what's appropriate for your particular altar. I have listed things here in what I consider their order of importance, and this represents what I keep upon my altar. Feel free to make up your own "welcomes" to things you place upon your altar that aren't listed here. Because this part of the ritual doesn't require a whole lot of actions, I've simply listed individual altar items and the words I use to welcome them.

Altar cloth: *May this cloth serve to protect and decorate my altar. By the power of the Lord and Lady, so mote it be!*

Goddess statue: *Lady, watch over the rites and magick I will practice here. May you ever guide my hand and heart. Blessed be!*

God statue: *Lord, I welcome you to this altar and my Witchcraft. Lend your power and wisdom to the rites performed here. Blessed be!*

Pentacle: *With this pentacle I symbolize the focal point of my altar. May it open to me the power of the gods and empower the work I do as a Witch. So mote it be!*

Athame: *May my athame ever serve my own true will and be welcome upon this altar. So mote it be!*

Wand: *With the wand, worlds are opened and magick is released. May it ever be charged and ready here. So mote it be!*

Chalice: *The love of the Goddess is expressed in the waters and wine of the chalice. May all who come to this altar never thirst. Blessed be!*

Cauldron: *From this cauldron magick shall be conjured up and destinies revealed. So mote it be!*

Candle: *Here the light of Witchcraft and the gods will shine upon my altar. Hail and welcome!*

Water dish: *The powers of water shall ever be a part of this working space. Hail the mysteries!*

Salt: *With the sacred salt of earth, we cleanse ourselves and our space. May its powers ever keep this altar safe and protected. So mote it be!*

Incense: *This incense shall bless and charge the rituals enacted here and the tools upon this altar. May the blessings of air surround us. Blessed be!*

Center candle: *And may the power of the All and the first cause ever bind the tools and powers gathered here. May this altar serve as a home to the powers I serve and the tools that serve me. So mote it be!*

A Coven Altar Blessing and Dedication (Jason)

Most of my ritual tools tend to be "twice blessed." They are blessed, dedicated, and consecrated in private, and then sometimes again with the coven. I think separate coven blessings for tools are especially important if a tool is going to be shared by several different people or an entire circle.

My wife and I host the activities of our coven, and as a result many of the tools and implements (I'm not really sure that a candle sconce counts as an official "Witch's tool") we use as a group "belong" to her and me in the sense that we paid for them and they stay with us. However, we want the members of our coven to feel as if they have some ownership of the tools we share and all use, which is why a dedication ritual for the altar is so important in the coven context.

Our working tools are designed to function as *an extension of our ourselves*, and a coven altar, as the center of a ritual, should function as *an extension of the coven*. The only way for something to function as an extension of the coven is for that tool to be blessed, dedicated, and consecrated by all those who are going to use it. The previous dedication ritual would probably work for a coven, but I think this one speaks better to the nature of a coven as a place of perfect love and chosen family.

This ritual requires an altar cloth (unless you aren't worried about scuff marks on your altar) and assumes that every covener owns an athame. If someone doesn't have an athame or forgets theirs the night of this rite, an index finger works just as well. If the altar you are dedicating is new, it should be cleansed before the ritual. I suggest using the first half of the previous dedication rite involving oil for this task. Once that is done, prepare your altar as usual for ritual and then cast the circle, call the quarters, and invoke the gods before beginning the rite.

High Priestess: *Hear ye, O coveners! We have come this night to bless and dedicate this altar for use in (coven name). May it serve as a gathering place for those who gather in perfect love and perfect trust, and a focal point for our magick! Around this altar we shall walk between the worlds and experience the power of the Lady and Lord. So mote it be!*

High Priest: *To properly bless and dedicate this altar, it must have all of our energies within it. For a coven is not just about those who lead, it is about all who meet here as chosen family. This altar shall be blessed and dedicated in the name of our coven and in the names of the Witches who circle around it!*

The high priestess should instruct all the coveners to grab their athames and then direct the coven to begin a fast walk going deosil (clockwise) to raise energy. Coveners should point their athames toward the altar as they walk, arms outstretched, athames in everyone's right hand so as not to poke anyone with a knife blade. As the circle begins to move, everyone should chant together:

This altar is ours, we do decree,
By Lord and Lady, so mote it be!

The chant should be repeated over and over again as the coven moves. Energy generally funnels upward when raised in a clockwise circle, and after chanting and circling for a few minutes the coven's energy should surround the altar. When the high priestess has determined that the energy has reached its peak, she should signal for the coven to stop and then direct everyone to place the tip of their athame upon the altar.

High Priestess: *The energy of this coven now surrounds our altar. It has felt our collective strength and spirit. A coven is one unit, but it is still a collection of individuals. This altar has felt OUR energy, but it also must feel each individual's energy so that it might truly serve us in our rites.*

High Priest: *Tonight we will share our individual energy with this altar so that all of us might resonate within it. We shall go around the circle and share a blessing, and while we do so we will all push a little bit of our individual energy out of ourselves and into the altar through our athames. And now I, (Witch name or mundane name of high priest), bless this altar with love and light. May it long be a gathering place for those who practice with (coven name). So mote it be!*

When the high priest is done, the person on his left should be instructed to share a blessing, and then so on clockwise until everyone has shared their energy with the altar. Individual coveners should feel free to make up their own blessing or repeat the one given here. If the coven uses a particular set of deities, even if it's just the Lady and Lord, their blessings should be invoked last, after the final covener has shared a blessing. If the coven doesn't have a particular set of deities they honor, the rite can end here with a hearty *So mote it be!*

High Priestess: *And now we ask our Lady and Lord (or names of specific deities) to bless this altar as we dedicate it to their service.*

High Priest: *Great God, be here with us in this place and upon this altar. May this altar serve as a sacred vessel for us to experience your blessings and power. Be welcome here. So mote it be!*

Everyone in the coven is then instructed to place the index and middle fingers of their dominant hand to their lips. As a group, they should kiss those fingers and then transfer that kiss to the statue of the God upon the altar. If there's no statue or other object representing the God, the kiss can simply be directed upward. After the kiss, the group should say together *So mote it be!* The kiss should be repeated a second time, this time with the kiss directed to the altar, with all coveners touching it. After the kiss, everyone should say *Blessed be!* The blessing is continued by the high priestess, who then invokes the Goddess in a similar manner.

High Priestess: *Gracious Goddess, be here with us in this place and upon this altar. Walk with us in this life and prepare us for the next. Bestow your blessings upon those who love you. Be welcome here in this circle and upon this altar. So mote it be!*

All coveners then share a kiss with the Lady as they did with the God, followed by another *So mote it be!* This is followed by one final kiss of the altar, signifying that the altar is a place worthy of celebrating the mysteries of the gods and Witchcraft. The rite ends with one final *Blessed be!*

LTAR-NATIVES
Altar and Moon Cake Recipes

Altar Cake

THIS IS A vegan-friendly cookie that makes a great altar cake and is easily imbued with the current season through the use of herbs and spices.

Ingredients

1 cup nuts (Any tree nut can be used. I like to use walnut post-Mabon and almond post-Ostara.)

1 cup oats

1 cup all-purpose flour

½ teaspoon baking powder

¼ teaspoon salt

Herbs or spices for your specific ritual (optional)

½ cup vegetable oil

½ cup maple syrup or honey (I use maple syrup post-Mabon and honey post-Ostara.)

1 tablespoon vanilla extract

Toast the nuts and let cool, then grind them with the oats for about fifteen seconds in a food processor until they are a mealy consistency.

Preheat the oven to 350°F.

Mix all dry ingredients together. If you are using herbs or spices for your specific ritual, add them now. Use ½ teaspoon of dried crushed herbs or ¼ teaspoon or less of spice, depending on the potency of your chosen spice. I pick an edible spice or herb that has the properties or associations I need for ritual.

I like to place the herb or spice on my altar for a week to charge it before use as well.

Mix the wet ingredients together, then combine wet and dry and mix well. The dough should be the consistency of thick mud. Place tablespoon dollops on a parchment-lined cookie sheet, with at least two inches between dollops.

Bake until golden brown.

These will be a crisp wafer cookie, and the recipe makes enough to share with friends and family.

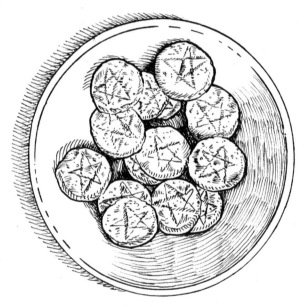

Altar cakes

Herb/Spice Blend Suggestions for Seasons and Rituals

Welcoming Spring Blend

¼ teaspoon dry mint

¼ teaspoon dry lavender

½ teaspoon lemon zest

Welcoming Summer Blend 1

⅓ teaspoon dry rose petals

¼ teaspoon powdered sage

Welcoming Summer Blend 2

If you have wild elderberry in your area, this combination makes a great summer blend.

1 tablespoon fresh elder blossoms

½ heaping teaspoon lemon zest

Welcoming Autumn Blend

¼ teaspoon dried thyme

⅓ teaspoon fresh rosemary, minced

½ teaspoon orange zest

Welcoming Winter Blend

$1/8$ teaspoon cinnamon

$1/8$ teaspoon nutmeg

$1/2$ teaspoon orange zest

$1/8$ teaspoon cardamom

Moon Cake

This recipe will make a crumbly cookie. It was developed for my coven by Sidney Eileen and sent to you with her permission.

Ingredients

$1½$ cups all-purpose flour

$1¼$ cups oats

$1/2$ teaspoon salt

$1/2$ teaspoon brown sugar

1 tablespoon honey

1 tablespoon white wine

$1/3$ cup unsalted butter

Preheat the oven to 350°F.

Mix the dry ingredients together. Mix the honey and wine together. Cut the butter into the dry ingredients, then add the honey-wine mixture. Form into balls and bake on a parchment-lined cookie sheet, leaving an inch or more between balls. Bake until lightly browned.

Diana Ewing

A Kitchen Witch in the tradition of her mother and grandmother, Diana blends food and drink with spells for her family, friends, and coven.

Sidney Eileen

Sidney Eileen is an artist, seamstress, writer, teacher, and ex-professional baker and pastry chef. A pagan witch since her youth, Sidney was given a list of ingredients a friend wanted used for the cakes for a full moon ritual more than a decade ago. She developed this recipe based on those ingredients and has used it ever since, sometimes adding other herbs and ingredients as appropriate for the time of year.

CHAPTER
SIX

Devotional Altars in Action
(Jason)

Many of the most important altars in my house are devotional altars dedicated to specific gods. The word *devotion* can be used in a multitude of ways, and every Witch's feelings about devotion to deity are going to be different. To some, devotion implies a sort of servitude toward the gods, but that's never been my experience. The Oxford Dictionary's primary definition of devotion is "love, loyalty, or enthusiasm for a person or activity," which sums up my relationship to the goddesses and gods in my life quite accurately. I love them, I'm loyal to them, and I have a lot of enthusiasm for them, and this is reflected on the altars in my house.

A devotional altar is primarily a place to pay your respects to a particular deity (or deities) and interact with that deity. For some people this might mean daily devotions and libations, while others might simply use the altar as a focus for prayer or meditation. My devotional altars are quite different from my primary working altar, generally because I don't use them for magickal work and they only rarely have any of my magickal tools on them. They also tend to be places for just my wife and me and seldom our coven.

Devotional altars are not limited to just gods and goddesses either. Many Witches keep devotional altars dedicated to their ancestors or perhaps a specific deceased family member. If there are any fey cohabitating in your home, then building them a devotional altar might be a wise choice as well, just to stay on their good side. Most of this chapter is going to focus primarily on devotional altars to deity, but the lessons and experiences shared here can apply to a variety of other situations.

In addition, the various types of altars we set up in our living spaces might reflect several different altar types. For example, an altar dedicated to the goddess Demeter might double as a seasonal altar, since Demeter is so readily identified with the harvest. What's most important about any sort of altar you set up is that it resonates with your experiences and honors the powers that are important to you.

Altars for One Deity or Spirit

I'm not sure the gods live at my house, but there are many deities that are close to my wife and me that at least have a guest bedroom. Because those deities are so important to us, they are often celebrated on our private devotional altars. Devotional altars dedicated to specific gods were some of the first altars I ever built outside of ritual as a Witch. As a devotee of the Greek god Pan, I've received a lot of "Pan stuff" over the years, things like panpipes, goat figurines, and phallic-shaped wands, and eventually it all collected in one place. I didn't mean for that collection of things to become an altar, but before long I found myself honoring Pan in that spot, turning it into a devotional altar.

Putting together an altar for a specific deity is extremely easy, and there's really no way to mess it up. What's important is finding things that remind you of and are associated with the deity you are choosing to honor—that's it. How you choose to go forward from there really is a matter of personal preference and/or divine inspiration.

The Greek Dionysus is one of the most revered and celebrated deities in our house, and his personal altar reflects his myth, our experiences with him, and what we know about him from history. His altar contains bottles of wine aged in clay vessels (instead of the more common wooden barrel), similar to the wine that would have been used to honor him in ancient Greece. Those bottles are flanked by two different statues of the god, with decorative bunches of grapes at the feet of both effigies. In addition to being a god of wine, Dionysus was also a god of the theater, and two masks we've used in ritual also sit upon that altar. A prized chalice adorns the center of our Dionysus altar (we need something to drink all that wine with!). When we think about Dionysus, we also think of the rock band The Doors, so there's also a bobble-head of Jim Morrison (their lead singer) on our altar.

Across from the Dionysus altar in our living room stands another devotional altar, this one for the goddess Aphrodite. Around four different statues of her, there's a collection of seashells we've acquired over the last few years from our favorite beach, along with an old sand dollar (which has a natural pentagram on it). Aphrodite was born in the Mediterranean Sea, so honoring her with things from the ocean feels natural. In the center of that altar is a bouquet of dried roses and my wife's first chalice (which was also her first ritual tool). There's no theological reason to have that chalice there, but it feels right for it to be there, so it is.

Many Witches build their devotional altars around a statue (or statues) of the god(s) they are honoring, but statues aren't necessary and can also be expensive. In the case of Dionysus, I'm sure he'd be happy enough being represented just by a wine bottle or a mask. I think a lot of us like statues though, because they provide a natural focus for the altar. It just feels more instinctive to direct my attention to a statue that looks like the god I'm honoring than to a wine bottle, but as Witches we do what we have to do.

I've often had people ask me just what a devotional altar is *for*. That's a very personal question, because devotional altars fill different needs for different Witches. I set them up to honor the gods I work with, kind of as a thank-you for being a part of my life. But I also set them up to serve as a focus for my devotions. It's often where I go to talk to them when I can't get outside (or don't have time to). At their devotional altars I feel their presence, which is what I cherish most.

Altars for Many Gods

Many Witches honor deities in tandem, like the Goddess and God, or perhaps an entire pantheon of deities, like the Hellenic or Egyptian gods. The gods of Witchcraft are virtually endless. If a deity calls to an individual Witch, that deity most likely deserves a place on the altar. However, the altar homes we give to our deities and spirits have to be carefully thought out. The powers and forces we honor are very real, and where and how we respect them matters.

Over the last couple of years, I've found myself deeply interested in the history of magick in the United States. This has led me to the spirit and legend of Marie Laveau (1801–1881), perhaps the most well-known occult figure in the history of the United States. I keep a small altar to Laveau in my office, but I keep it well away from all of my traditional Witch regalia and the Pagan gods I honor. I do that because in addition to being a Voodoo priestess, Laveau was also a practicing Catholic. (The two belief systems are not mutually exclusive.) To set the statues I have of her next to Pan or Dionysus would be disrespectful.

I don't believe "the gods" (or spirits) think in exactly the same way that you or I do, but their myths tell us that they have some preferences. Zeus's wife Hera was never a fan of his philandering ways and often punished her husband by tormenting his children. Much of the myth of Hercules is based on Hera's cruelty to her husband's son. Because of that, I keep Zeus and Hera apart on my altars.

If you are putting together a devotional altar for a variety of deities, make sure those deities get along and are used to being honored in the context of Witchcraft. The gods of the Norse, Greeks, Celts, Babylonians, and Egyptians have been sharing space for centuries now. (In the ancient world, deities from different pantheons would often show up together in art and in temples. This continued when Western-style Paganism was reborn in occult groups such as the Golden Dawn in the nineteenth century.) Before setting up a shared altar, checking the compatibility of the deities that will share that altar is a must.

Setting the Italian Witch goddess Aradia next to Pan on a shared altar makes perfect sense. The two deities have been associated with each other for the last hundred years, and Aradia's mother was the Roman Diana (the Greek Artemis).

They have a pretty high degree of intersectionality. By way of comparison, Aradia and the Native American (most likely Hopi) Kokopelli have almost nothing in common, and the idea of placing those two deities together brings up issues of cultural appropriation and disrespect toward Native practices.

There are times when we just have to trust the little voices in our head and the whispers we hear on the wind. If we believe in deities, then we also have to believe that they can communicate with us. If Aradia lets me know that she wants a place on one of my altars next to the Norse Thor, even though this makes absolutely no sense to me, I'm going to go ahead and do it.

When setting up a shared altar, I tend to build that altar around whatever shared theme has brought those deities together. In the spring and early summer that shared theme might be love, lust, and fertility. At our house that often means Pan and Aphrodite surrounded by flowers, womb-like chalices, and phallic-shaped wands and athames. Though the two deities together are expressing a shared idea, I like to give them both a "sphere of influence" on the altar.

A springtime altar for Pan and Aphrodite will have a few acorns and oak leaves on Pan's side of things. (The oak is sacred to the land he was born in, Greek Arcadia.) On Aphrodite's side, my wife might leave a piece of jewelry, since we know she likes pretty things. We always try to acknowledge

Devotional Altars in Action

the individual nature of the gods we place together. Just like we don't all like the same things, the gods don't either.

Finding Time for Love: Spell from Our Aphrodite Altar

My wife works a very stressful job that keeps her away from our home for up to twenty-four hours at a time. The life of a Pagan writer isn't quite so hectic, but I often find my brain and attention focused completely on altars (like right now) and other witchy odds and ends. The end result of all of this is that we often find ourselves not spending enough quality time together, and when that happens we visit our home's Aphrodite altar.

We believe that the gods benefit when we experience the emotions and pleasures we associate with them. In the case of Aphrodite, this means she wants our love to be as deep and fulfilling as possible, and she wants us to have time to explore that love. She especially likes it if that exploration gets a little, umm, physical. Not only does she just seem like the perfect goddess to ask for such an assist, but we think she's got a vested interest in it.

This is a spell that can be adapted for a variety of needs as well. It could be done to carve out more time with a friend or family member, or even for a hobby or personal interest. Just make sure that whoever you are trying to bring closer wants to be closer! If your best friend Doug no longer wants to hang out with you, a spell might help with that, but it would be pretty darn unethical.

This spell requires two candles and some altar space. We use our devotional altar to Aphrodite when we perform it, but any altar will work. If you want to add a little extra oomph to this spell, I suggest an offering to Aphrodite (red wine is what we use most), along with some rose petals. The rose petals double as another gift to Aphrodite and serve as another layer to the spell (though they aren't necessary).

For the purposes of this spell, we always start with an invocation to Aphrodite. We know that she's generally around our altar when we call to her, but it's best to start any petition to the gods with praise, thanks, and an explanation as to what you want:

> *Gracious Aphrodite, goddess of love and pleasure, thank you for being a part of our lives and for all the blessings you've given us over the years. We come to you tonight with the hope that you can bring us even closer together and help us to share our time and energy with each other. Bless this work tonight that it might benefit not only our relationship but also our devotion to you. So mote it be!*

At this point we prefer to leave Aphrodite an offering, simply to thank her for the attention she's giving us. If you are uncomfortable with offerings, just skip this part and move on to the next. I think it's best to be as explicit as possible with offerings, such as offering a hearty *To you, my Lady!* before placing the wine or whatever else you might be using in the offering bowl. If you are using something like wine, you can take a sip too. Think of it as sharing a toast.

Aphrodite spell

Now you and your partner should each take a candle and put some intention into it. See yourself in your mind's eye with the person you are trying to find time for, and doing the things you want to be doing with them. They should do the same with their candle. (If you do an adapted version of this ritual, you can do this for each candle. The other half of the spell's focus doesn't necessarily have to be present for it to work. In addition, if finding personal time is your obstacle, you might work on the spell in the afternoon, with your partner finishing it up when they get home.)

Once the candles are charged, place them on opposite ends of the altar, facing each other. If you have some rose petals, sprinkle them on top of your altar while saying:

Great Aphrodite, may your blessings rain upon us, and may we find the time we need for our love to thrive. By your hand and power, let our relationship fire, spark, and be alive! With harm to none, we ask this boon of you. So mote it be!

If you don't have any rose petals, simply pretend to sprinkle them on the altar, letting the energy of your intention fall from your fingertips.

Return to your Aphrodite altar every day after the ritual, repeating the request for her blessings and sprinkling the rose petals and/or energy. Then light your personal candle for one hour. When the hour is up, blow it out and move the candle an inch or two toward the center of the altar. Your partner should do the same with their candle. The spell ends when the candles are finally touching each other or Aphrodite has granted your wish. If the candles haven't burned down completely, light them one final time in honor of Aphrodite, and leave her one final offering.

Devotional Altars in Action

The Care and Feeding of the Gods: Offerings, Devotions, and Sacrifice

For many of us, devotional altars are not just places for devotion, but are places to leave devotions. In *Witchcraft Today*, Gardner wrote that the Witches he knew "believed in gods who were not all-powerful" (chap. 10). Many Witches believe that our relationships with deity should be reciprocal. Certainly they are beings with more power than us, but they benefit when we pray to, worship, and honor them. We also give them power when we leave them things.

For some Witches, leaving gifts to the gods serves to demonstrate their devotion to a specific deity or deities. Giving the Morrigan a few sips of your favorite whisky shows that you love and appreciate her. At our house we often pour a little wine out for Dionysus, either in our yard or in a chalice on his altar. Does he actually drink this wine like you or I would? Of course not. But we believe that the essence of it goes to him as it is absorbed into the earth or evaporates in the chalice.

Some Witches leave offerings as a thank-you to the deities they honor and ask assistance from. If Aphrodite helps you to find the love of your life, why not leave her a rose as a thank-you gift? There are also certain deities who expect payment after helping a follower. The gods aren't all necessarily love and light. Like human beings, they value appreciation and thanks, and they don't exist for us to boss them around.

When they help us out of a tight situation, we should give them something in return.

If you've set up a devotional altar to a specific deity (or deities), that's an ideal place to leave them offerings. It's a space that has been established as a spot where they are welcome and might possibly reside. Instead of taking an offering outside to a place where you don't generally do ritual, that offering should go where your connection with a given deity is strongest. When I first began leaving devotional offerings on one of my personal altars, I found the practice a bit odd (What's going to happen to this cupcake in three days?), but now it has become second nature.

The most common types of things left for the gods are food and drink. Even the simplest drinks have a lot of power; humans can last a month without food, but only three days without water. But food and drink are only the beginning when it comes to altar offerings. Just about anything that feels right to you can be left as an offering. Money, stones, and written prayers are all pretty common but aren't necessarily better than anything else. Sometimes a deity will provide some instruction as to what their preferences are, and when that happens it's a suggestion that should be followed.

When offering a liquid offering to one of my gods, I generally do two things. One is to splash a few drops of the offering on a statue (or a representative object) of the deity. Sometimes I'll take this a step further and brush a few drops of the liquid directly onto the statue's mouth. (I do this most often with alcoholic beverages.) While I don't think my Santa Muerte statue is actually Santa Muerte, I believe that the goddess (and Catholic folk saint) resides at least to a small degree within it. Mythology tells us that the gods generally like earthly things, so why not make sure they get those things?

Once I've shared a few sips of drink, I leave the rest of the drink on my altar to evaporate. Often that drink is poured into a specific bowl set up for such things on my altar, but sometimes I'll just leave a shot of whisky in a shot glass for the gods too. It's a lot like taking a shot with a friend, except the gods don't throw their liquor back as quickly as we humans do. After the drink has evaporated, I'll then wash out the bowl (or shot glass) that held it, making sure to thank the deity that had the drink for their love and assistance in my life.

Drinks are probably my favorite thing to leave, because there's very little clean-up or smell involved, but sometimes you might find yourself wanting to share some food with a particular deity. Food presents a few more challenges, because we know that it won't evaporate and will probably be on our altar until we remove it. Because of this I generally only use food as an offering when it's food I really like (no deity wants that can of peas you don't want to eat), and I generally give only a small amount. I love cupcakes, which means they are a great offering item. They are also small, and one cupcake is not going to smell in twelve hours or attract an army of ants.

So keep your food offerings small and perhaps also quick. If you feel the need to share some of your dinner with a deity, perhaps it should be left on your altar only for the time it takes you to eat dinner. The gods are a very real part of our lives, so why not treat them like revered family members?

The gods don't "eat" in the same sense that we do. Instead they draw the life-giving essence out of the food we leave for them. This has led many people to avoid eating any food left on an altar for the gods. While I don't think the gods will curse you if you eat something you set aside for them, I generally don't advise doing it either. I'm not a huge fan of throwing offerings directly into the garbage can, but if an object won't decompose, that's probably where it should go. How a person feels about using the garbage can as a receptacle for used offerings will vary from Witch to Witch.

If you've got a compost pile, that's the best place to leave the offerings you've given, and the one I think the gods would be most inclined to appreciate. Another alternative is to burn them in a fire, like a burnt offering. This option is especially useful if the god you've given an offering to is a jealous deity. (Some goddesses and gods just don't like to share.) If your gods get along nicely with one another, a shared designated spot outside near a tree or bush works well. Crossroads are traditional places to take offerings in practices such as Conjure, and any other liminal space works well too.

Many physical objects besides food can be disposed of in similar ways, but some things are more problematic than others. If I leave money as an offering, I certainly don't want to throw it into a fire or the compost pile. Instead I take it to a shopping center and "accidentally" drop it on the ground, assuming that it will eventually end up in the hands of whoever the gods desire. Another way of getting rid of money when left as an offering is to let it accumulate on the altar (generally in a box or bowl) and then donate it to a charity approved of by the deity it was left for.

Offerings are not the same thing as sacrifices, either. We give offerings to the gods to show our respect and our thanks. It's not something we are generally obligated to do, and in the Charge of the Goddess we are directly told that the gods of Witchcraft "do not demand sacrifice." If making an offering means you won't be able to pay your rent or will go hungry, it's not worth doing. But most of us can spare a little beer and a piece of dessert.

Physical items aren't the only thing we can leave to the gods on their altar. It's the exchange of energy that's important to many of us, and that can be accomplished without food, drink, or coinage. In my experience, the gods appreciate prayers and praise, and that's something we all can give to the Lord and Lady with ease.

Reading a poem you've written to a particular god is a powerful offering, and the reading of that poem will give them strength and vitality. Just saying a deity's name can have an effect, and will be appreciated. If you feel silly reading or saying something out loud at your devotional altar, write your offering on a sheet of paper and slip it under their statue or whatever you are using to represent them. This will give them energy too!

A reciprocal relationship with the gods is about giving them energy when they lend their energies to our rites and spellcraft. Just how we give them that energy is immaterial, as long as we do it. The Witch's altar is a powerful place to facilitate that give-and-take, and what you can give to the gods is nearly limitless.

LTAR-NATIVES

Sacrifice in New Orleans Voodoo:
A Larger View in a Shrinking World

WE ARE ALL part of a vast community. We stand in relation, in intimate relationship, to the boundless expanse that surrounds and nurtures us. This unimaginable field of things and beings is connected through a reciprocity that is the very flow of the elixir of life. This give-and-take connects the visible and invisible worlds. The spirits, loa, goddesses, and gods need us as much as we need them. Sacrifice is the sacrament, the celebration, of all of our sacred connectedness.

A sacrifice can be made in two ways. There is the sacrifice of some "object/other" and the sacrifice of the "self." Underlying these two options is a basic understanding that defines the act of sacrifice as "to make sacred" (from the Latin *sacer*, "sacred," and *facere*, "to make"). This sacredness completes and reaffirms the grace of the world (*mundus*, or "world"). Brilliant starlight plays within the deeps of the world, illuminating that which it recognizes as none other than itself. There is a flexible completeness rather than a stiff hierarchy.

Sacrifice of some object/other brings benefit to both the practitioner and the recipient. This object/other can take the form of an object (money, gold, a talisman, some food item favored by the spirit, etc.) or of some other (a being; a life form, as the term is understood by the practitioner). When offering an object, give something the recipient spirit wants and enjoys. How the sacrifice is made can outweigh what is given, particularly if you are not sure of the spirit's tastes. Honor and respect always sweeten the pot.

Great care is called for in the sacrifice of another life form. It is here that the shrinking world has impacted my and many other voodoos in their practices. With the present-day accessibility of Eastern spiritual practices, in particular Tibetan Buddhism, came the "kind mother" teaching. Concisely put, given an infinite number of incarnations, every sentient being we meet has at one time been our kind mother. To take the life of a being that at one point in time loved and nurtured us is dishonorable. Mammals are usually the first to come to mind as life forms, but if you consider trees or flowers to be life forms with sentience, then the simple act of picking a flower to be used as an offering would best be preceded by careful consideration.

Lastly, it is important to write of sacrifice in relation to the self. Here we move from majick to mysticism. The purpose of majick is usually prediction and control. A sacrifice is made to an entity, and the practitioner gains the assistance of the entity in predicting and/or controlling events, circumstances, or other persons. In mysticism, the practitioner sacrifices a perceived self in order to strip bare an underlying, more primary true identity. "Know thyself" is the key element here. The Spider Rites performed in the early 1980s are an example of this type of sacrifice. In these rites, participants offered themselves as food to astral spiders. What was left after the rite was an essential, indestructible Self.

Louis Martinié
**Louis Martinié is the content editor
at Black Moon Publishing.**

CHAPTER SEVEN

Outdoor Altars
(Tempest)

s there anything more Pagan than an altar outdoors? Probably at the mere mention of the words *altar* and *outdoors* your brain is already conjuring up images of Stonehenge and other monoliths—or perhaps a secret grotto with a half-hidden statue of a goddess, with flowers and other offerings strewn about in front of her, and the sounds of rustling leaves and chirping birds. Just being in nature can be a religious experience!

Crafting an outdoor altar can be very satisfying, though there are a host of other things to consider that you don't have to worry about with an indoor altar. The biggest thing to consider is the weather and other side effects of being out in the elements. Another is security, concerning other humans as well as wildlife interfering with your altar. Privacy can also be an issue, depending on the style and size of your rituals and the proximity of your neighbors to the altar. Outside altars can also require a lot more upkeep—which is not a bad thing either. It can actually be a challenge to yourself to maintain it, versus an indoor altar that you may forget about.

Creating Permanent Altars

If you have the time, money, muscle, interest, and land to create a permanent outdoor altar, then basically the sky (and everywhere it falls on your property) is the limit. Outdoor altars are definitely a never-ending labor of love, which makes them a wonderful way to be continually active at your altar and connect with the outdoors at the same time. You can ask any Witch who has an outdoor altar or shrine, and they will tell you it's a work in progress, always. This is good to keep in mind if you're just starting out and wondering when it will finally be finished. It won't be! That's the beautiful thing about an altar that is essentially living—growing and dying with the seasons, and by the work of your own hands.

How far you'd like to go in creating your outdoor altar is up to you. Some Witches make extravagant grottoes, circles within circles, labyrinths, full-size shrines, stone-offering slabs and structures, fire pits, ponds, and memorials in their yard spaces. Others focus on a small area of the yard that doesn't seem out of the ordinary to the non-practitioner. So the best location depends on your needs, desires, the property itself, and the neighborhood. If you like the idea of an outdoor altar but are unsure of what you want, start researching and visiting parks, gardens, and sacred sites—and take notes and pictures! Scour the internet for inspiration, and save those images and ideas in a folder. Check out your local garden center to see if they offer any classes or free lectures on what grows best in your area.

There are two main factors to think about when making an outdoor altar. It's very important to avoid getting carried away with a fantasy that won't thrive or function properly for your needs. The first thing to consider is that you are creating a living environment. The second factor to remember is that you need to craft a workable space. These two things will directly affect how successful your efforts will be.

Creating a living environment means thinking sustainably and long term. Pay careful attention to what planting zone you live in, the native flora and fauna, and characteristics of the landscape. The plant hardiness zone will tell you what plants will work best for where you live, so you can invest wisely in what you grow. For example, palm trees don't thrive in the Northeast, but I have seen many people try (and fail) to make it happen. Investigate what is native to your area. Again, your local community garden center can help point you in the right direction so you can avoid planting invasive or inappropriate species. They can also tell you which plants attract wildlife or

Witches gathered at an outdoor altar

repel pests. Understanding the features of your land is also vital: note sections that are sunny/shady, prone to flooding, or at risk of erosion. Essentially these are landscaping basics, but if you want a bower with vines to cover your altar or form a grove, you need to know what grows best.

Crafting a workable space also takes a fair amount of planning, but generally, once you've done the initial work, you just have to maintain it. Consider what you need for your practices. Do you need a large area of flat ground for ten people to do ritual on? If so, will that mean having dirt, gravel, pavement, or grass? Wood chips are cheap but are hard to dance on, and they collect on cloak bottoms—and dirt can turn to mud. If it's just you, then you may not need a large, clear space. Do you want a fire pit? If so, what are the fire regulations for your area? How close to buildings can the pit be? Are you looking to make a contained space for a bonfire, or do you want a small raised stone caldera to make offerings in? What height does your altar need to be so it is comfortable for your workings? What is the best surface for your work, and what's easiest to clean up?

Weather is going to be a big factor. Do you have to worry about freezing temperatures or excessive rain or heat? Will you need shade or some kind of shelter, and is that something nature can help you provide, or will you have to build it? Consider what materials will last the longest where you live. Ceramic pots seem really durable and earthy, but if you live where the temperature can hit freezing, you may find them shattered. Glass containers holding liquid can explode as well. Concrete and wood containers are better options for those zones. Ceramics as decoration (tiles, statues, etc.) that aren't going to be holding earth or water are generally safe. Resin can be worn down quickly by high temperatures and long-term exposure to the sun but can last longer in temperate places. Cast plaster will definitely erode quickly when exposed to wetness. Metals such as copper, bronze, iron, and steel can be really durable, but they also get very hot quickly just sitting in the sun. Stone tends to be the most durable material all around, though certain types can be slippery when wet!

It may be wise to consult a landscaper/builder so you can choose the best materials for your weather and your budget. Whether you're investing in plants, containers, garden features, or statuary for your altar, be sure to *ask* if what you're buying is suitable for where it will go.

Creating Outdoor Altars for Renters and Those with Small Spaces

For many of us who rent, the idea of having a permanent outdoor space is just a beautiful dream. When you're renting your home, you're not going to want to invest a whole lot of time and money in a property that isn't yours—even if you have permission to do so! It's a constant pull between beautifying the space for your own tastes, upholding landlord expectations, and knowing that whatever investments you do make are essentially sunk cost. Or if you're sharing outdoor space with other neighbors, they may not respect or appreciate your efforts.

But there are ways to craft your space—even if it's temporary or limited or you don't want to make it obvious that you're a Witch.

Potted plants: Obviously these are portable and can symbolize earth. A small container of earth can make a great altar to bury intentions and other spellcraft in, or leave offerings on (even without a plant). You can also choose a plant that is sacred to a deity you work with, such as a rose plant for Aphrodite.

Rocks and crystals: These magnify energy and also represent earth, without you having to worry about growing anything. You can also use them to accent pots and mark quarters.

Water: If you are aligned with the element of water, then having a water feature of some sort may be your ideal altar. You can use a birdbath or a small fountain—ideal for small porches where you have access to electricity to run a pump.

Wind and wings: If you work with air, there are a multitude of wind chimes to choose from—metal, bamboo, glass, ceramic, etc.—and you can even fashion your own out of old silverware! If you must have quiet, then hang a flag that represents your deity. (You can make one or order one online.) You could also get a birdfeeder to create a haven (along with your birdbath). Hummingbird feeders are less messy because you don't have to worry about seeds—and the other creatures that want to eat them.

Tiny fires: Fire makes a great altar, but it's problematic for small spaces. You could use solar-powered LED lanterns or candles if actual fire is an issue and the purpose of your flame is mainly devotional. Otherwise there are an array of fire pots, such as chimeneas and metal and stone fire pits, that are safe and easy to move. Just mind your fire codes!

Altar furniture: Keep an eye out for small tables that are designed for weathering the outdoors. Treated wood trays, metal and tile plant stands, and decorative tables all make excellent altars—and look lovely as well! So even if you only have a few feet of space on a patio or porch, you can easily create an outdoor sanctuary for yourself.

Tempest's Backyard Shrine

As much as I would like to consider myself a Green Witch, that truly does not seem to be my calling in life. I can't have plants indoors because our cats see it as a personal challenge to kill them. It's hard to have a proper outdoor garden altar because my partner and I travel a lot. But I sure do try! For things I want to focus on growing, I use large pots and containers to keep them hydrated and relatively free of weeds. For everything else, I pretty much let nature do her thing.

Much of what grows at our home is what my mother-in-law calls a "volunteer garden." Interestingly enough, the self-planted varieties include a lot of poisonous plants, such as foxglove, woody nightshade (two different kinds), wormwood, bluebells, and hemlock—plus a host of mints, rosemary, lamb's ear, lavender, and more. Plants aside, I've created an altar area out of marble slab scraps, making an alcove area on top of a low fence that's about chest-high. Around the marble I've built a bower out of branches and trained morning glory and another kind of groundcover vine to go on top of it. Within its shelter is an outdoor-suitable resin statue of a nature goddess. Around her I've placed stones that I've pulled up out of the yard, as well as shells, stones, and crystals I've collected on our travels. Before the altar are two large flowerpots with blooming plants, and to the sides are more herbs. There is enough clearance from plants that I can place candles or light

Tempest's backyard shrine

torches without setting anything on fire. I try to tend to the altar regularly and leave offerings as I come across interesting things.

The only cost involved in my outdoor shrine was the statue itself, which I found in a catalog on sale for under fifty dollars. Being an artist, I am sorely tempted to create something out of fired clay or some other durable material, but I don't have the time right now—or the additional funds to rent a ceramics studio to do the work. Everything else for the altar I found or was given to me. A bounty of free building materials (wood, bricks, stone, fixtures, pottery, and much more) can be found on the free section of Craigslist, just for making the effort of contacting someone and picking up the stuff. Heck, I've had free slabs of concrete delivered by builders who just wanted it gone! Keeping an eye out at yard sales, flea markets, and salvage yards can also score you great materials for a fraction of the cost.

It frustrates me when people say, "Oh, I could never afford to do that." Isn't a huge part of Witchcraft focusing your will and your intent? By saying you can't do a thing, you're not going to get much further because you're defeating yourself. When I started out, I thought to myself, "I want to build an outdoor shrine," and slowly but surely it began to manifest. I kept an eye out and an ear open, but I also suddenly had friends who didn't even know my plan offering me things that worked perfectly. If it's a matter of physical labor, see what you can trade or barter for help to make it happen. If you're part of a group and the altar is going to be something everyone uses, get everyone on board and do a potluck work day. Be a Witch. Do the thing.

The Great Outdoors and Sacred Sites

While I would love to make a detailed list of sacred sites you can visit, this really isn't the book for it. Instead we're going to focus on the protocol of visiting sacred sites, as well as opening your eyes to ones already around you. We often think of sacred sites as old or ancient, and often natural—and maybe rapidly disappearing. These things can all be true, but new sites can and are being created around, for, and by us.

Visiting Sites and Personal Responsibility

When visiting sacred sites, it's necessary to consider your own impact on the space. Some places are designed to be participatory: you are instructed or encouraged by the caretakers to make an offering, interact with the space, leave something behind, make a mark, etc. At other sites anything like that is strictly forbidden, and it's crucial to be respectful of those rules. Many sites have been harmed because people didn't listen and figured it was okay to take just one pebble or stone, pick a flower, carve a symbol, etc. But the effect of these "just one" actions multiplied by hundreds and thousands of hands and feet over time adds up. It can truly have an impact that leads to the space being damaged or less preserved for future generations.

This also applies to lesser known places, shrines, and special spots that are off the beaten path. If you're going to do spellwork or leave an offering at such a place, make sure it's biodegradable and won't cause damage to the site or any animals. Synthetic ribbons, plastic items, candles, glitter, metal pieces, etc., can create serious problems for flora and fauna. Seeds of plants that are invasive species should be left at home. Be careful about rearranging the natural environment in order to make a mark for your ego. You could be damaging the habitat of species you can't even see. Don't be that person.

Also be aware that if you're leaving regular food offerings, particularly in wild areas, you can unintentionally cause local animals to become accustomed to it, which may put them in danger. In the city it's a bit of a different matter, but it's still something to be mindful of. I live in a neighborhood in Seattle famous for its population of crows, and I do give them offerings on occasion. Not far from where I live, a little girl had been feeding the crows regularly, and they started leaving her gifts in return. However, not everyone in the neighborhood was so appreciative, and some complained. Luckily Seattle tends to be a very environmentally conscious city (and

I believe the neighbors were told to get over it), but other places may use poisons and other harmful methods to "control" the population. Another thing about city living that many people forget is that the city is host to a wide variety of creatures—skunks, raccoons, squirrels, possums, rabbits, rats, and even coyotes—in addition to pets gone feral, so food will attract them. If you're not willing to deal with all of the other creatures your food offerings may attract, then you should reconsider your method of delivery.

LTAR-NATIVES

Place Altars

EVER SINCE I was very young, I've had a strong sense of place. Whether it was the big juniper tree that became my first outdoor hiding place or the many wild and beautiful hikes in the Columbia River Gorge that I've explored as an adult, I've never met a place in nature that I didn't fall in love with. And as a naturalist pagan, my deepest connection is to the physical level of nature itself. So my altar celebrates those places that I've bonded with particularly deeply, even if it was just for one visit.

This "place altar" is literally a map of those locations. In the center are a few sacred items that represent me and my world: a ceramic wolf jug I made in high school, a couple of sacred necklaces, and a few other spiritual trinkets. And then arrayed around it are rocks, twigs and other items I've brought home from my travels. Each item is labeled with the place it's from and the date it was collected. While the space is too small to make everything perfectly to scale, I do create a map showing where, relative to here, each piece came from.

I tend to watch the ground a great deal when I am walking, so when I am at a particularly special place I keep my eyes peeled for just the right memento to present itself to me. I'll know it when I see it, and my suspicions are always confirmed as soon as I pick it up and feel a distinct *yes* or *no*. In some cases, such as in state parks, I'm not able to take anything from the land itself, but I may pick up something I find in the parking lot or on a nearby road. Gift shops have also offered up suitable altar items.

Since I no longer practice magic, I don't use the altar for any sort of ritual. Rather, it's a daily reminder of all the amazing places I've been introduced to. Moreover, it strengthens my resolve to care for the land, particularly with all the damage we've done to it. My sacred acts are those of physical restoration and education, and my place altar is a microcosm of everything that's at stake. However, you can certainly create a place altar to be used for rituals celebrating and helping the land and its beings.

You don't need anything fancy to start a place altar. Any flat surface will do, though be aware that organic materials such as sticks will degrade over time in an outdoor space. Then, as you go to various places that are particularly sacred to you, collect appropriate items to represent them. You may find that the place shows you exactly what you need, while other times you may have to do a little hunting around. Please only take something very small, and never take any living being, whether animal, plant (including flowers), or fungus. If you feel moved to leave a gift, make a donation to the nearest park facility or conservation group.

Lupa
Lupa is a naturalist pagan author, artist, and citizen scientist in the Pacific Northwest. She may be found online at www.thegreenwolf.com.

A great way to get immersed in the outdoors and to consider the sacred is to see it with a child's eyes. It's never too early to teach our children how to recognize their own connection to the world and the divine. Next, Gwion provides some wonderful tips on how to share the great outdoors with offspring.

LTAR-NATIVES

Building Altars with Our Children

ALTARS HAVE ALWAYS been a pretty big deal in our house. There are altars on practically every flat surface, and they are tended to regularly. Ever since our children were quite small, they participated in making altars for holidays, ancestors, and pieces of magic being worked by the whole family.

Creating altars with our kids was simple because mostly it centered around activities we were doing anyway, like decorating the house for Yule or celebrating the changing seasons. As boxes of decorations were pulled out of the garage or the magical tools cabinet, our son and daughters started placing meaningful items in special places. Before too long those "special places" became traditions, and now certain items *always* go in just that same spot. My kids will say things like, "Because, Dad, we always put the goddess on the windowsill."

Fashioning altars that honor the turning of the seasons is probably where we started. For me, connecting to the natural world and its rhythms is vitally important. According to my kids, if I don't get outside on a regular basis to take a long hike or stroll by the river or visit the beach, I get grumpy. Of course, what they are just beginning to realize is that they get grumpy too. (Sneaky dad wins the day!)

Although the methods for creating seasonal altars will differ according to wherever you are, there are a few basics that seem to be pretty global. Here's what we've done. Modify as needed for your area.

Step One: Go Outside

I know this step sounds ridiculously basic, but it's quite foundational. Scents change as the seasons change. Different plants blossom and tantalize our olfactory senses. As leaves grow or fall from trees, the light shifts, casting shadows or altering the view. If you are outside enough, you'll begin to notice when these changes occur.

A side note: I grew up in a busy industrial city with a working port system. On hot days, the asphalt smelled like diesel fuel. After it rained, the streets had a peculiar smell of oil, diesel, and fresh rain. I still associate that concoction of odors with rain. So noticing changes doesn't have to be all about flowers and butterflies.

Step Two: Acknowledge the Changes

I'd often chat with my children about the differences they noticed. Why does the meadow look different today? What does the smell on the wind remind you of? How should we dress today? What has grown or withered?

Step Three: Collect Things

This is where the fun really begins. We've gathered acorns, pine cones, broken tree branches without leaves and lots of attached moss, bottle tops, rocks, toy parts, photographs, dead fish…you name it. (Note: Dead fish from a dried-up seasonal pond= least favorite altar ever!) We'd pick up whatever the kids wanted to collect that represented to them just how the world was in that exact moment.

Step Four: Make Altars

I've mostly left the particulars up to my children, but suggestions I would make run along these lines:

- Indoor or outdoor altar? (See note about the dead fish.)
- Do we need other items, like a table or an altar cloth, or are we good with what we have?
- How will we tend to this altar?
- Is our altar going to keep growing if we collect more things on our next walk?
- Is there a story, spirit of place, or deity associated with this altar that we want represented?
- How will we know when it's time to take this altar down?

Step Five: Return the Altar from Whence It Came

Everything has its time. Summer gives way to autumn, flowers wither, and I won't even begin to tell you what happened with that fish! Knowing when to take down an altar or change it up or put it away is as important as constructing it in the first place.

Step Six: Repeat as Often as the Kids Want To

We've built altars for everything, and an interesting thing has happened along the way: our kids build and use altars for themselves now. As they've grown, altar building has grown with them. School projects, life dreams, relationship break-ups, a new home, and friends or relatives who have passed through the veil all get altars.

It's part of who they are now. They know when it's time to grieve or plan or contemplate or celebrate and when it's time to move on, because they know how to create altars.

Gwion Raven
Gwion Raven is a Priestess, Witch, and teacher.
www.tobeawitch.com

Sacred Sites, the Fey, and Other Kinfolk

Many places that are designated as sacred sites have a long history of being associated with the fey and other similar folk. From mountaintops in New England Native American lore and rocks in Iceland that are said to be the domain of such beings to wells and trees in the United Kingdom that are said to be visiting spots or gateways, the stories and sites abound. It seems like our ancestors' first instinct at most of these places was to avoid these spirits, but as we cover more and more of the planet, we're invading their space—and they ours in return. This clash can be very problematic, to say the least, when handled without respect and understanding. However, there have been plenty of times when we and the other kin have coexisted harmoniously. A balanced and respectful state can be achieved when we pay attention.

Thanks largely to the Victorians, when most people hear or see the word *fairy*, they think of pretty, happy flower fairies, Tinker Bell, and other cute things. But most Witches who actually know, have worked with, or otherwise have been exposed to the fey know otherwise. Rather than thinking of them as imaginary or childlike, we should give them the respect we would offer to anyone from a different culture or place. They are people too; just a different kind—with real consequences. There's a reason why actual lore about the fey are often cautionary tales with lots of warnings to heed in order to be both safe and respectful. Think about the cultural barriers and differences that are involved when visiting a foreign country: language, customs, and laws. To enter another country without considering these things would be rude, irresponsible, and potentially dangerous. Now apply that sensibility to the fey and similar folk, and you'll be on your way to a much better understanding of them.

Creating little doors along buildings in surprising places and crafting tiny houses in the yard is all about amusing ourselves. I want to be very clear: there's absolutely nothing wrong with that. But these places are not crafted for the fey. The fey are not going to live or "play" in these spots. They're basically acts at the Altar of Imagination. We may create such things to challenge our own perceptions, maintain our own sense of play, keep offspring busy, attempt to reenchant the world, and also consider other worlds and realms.

But if you truly wish to work with the fey, there are better ways to go about it. A proper shrine to the fey and similar folk requires allocating space for them. Having an untouched section of your yard where you let nature do its thing is one way to honor them. You can also leave offerings that they will find appealing at the edge of such spaces. The fey don't need us to manufacture homes for them; they were here before us, and plenty of similar folk already coexist with us in our own homes—which has led to much lore about house spirits. The key thing to remember is to show them respect.

LTAR-NATIVES

Creating a Backyard Faery Altar

THERE ARE SEVERAL benefits to creating a faery altar. The fae can impart a sense of wonder to your daily life, and their ethereal energy can elevate your magical practice to a higher realm.

One of the best places for a faery altar is your own backyard. Find a place such as a tree trunk or a little out-of-the-way nook. It shouldn't be too sunny or shady and shouldn't be anywhere near the lawn mower's path. It also shouldn't be visible from the road. Clear away any weeds or rocks, and level the ground with some additional dirt or sand if needs be. Cleanse the space energetically by burning white sage or palo santo.

Look for natural items for your faery altar. Opt for items made of ceramic, glass, wood, and metal. You may want to buy flowerpots or plant bulbs to bookend the altar. Fragrant herbs such as lavender, sage, and mint also attract the wee ones.

Perhaps the best items for a faery altar are a couple of clear quartz crystals. I recommend buying new ones from your favorite Pagan store, just to make sure the energy is fresh.

Other must-have items for your faery altar are tiny, dedicated dishware for offerings. A small plate, such as a soy sauce bowl, is perfect for holding a couple of strawberries or pieces of chocolate. A shot glass is likewise perfect for a beverage offering, such as mead, juice, or wine.

Consider buying faery figurines. Faeries are immensely attracted to them, even if they don't exactly resemble them. Glass globes, or "faery balls," can be a lovely addition as well, as long as they aren't too big. Ceramic or metal mushrooms are also a big hit.

Once you have everything for your altar, arrange your items beautifully. Keep a little space between the objects so the altar doesn't feel too crowded. Lastly, hang ribbons and wind chimes from branches, so they blow and tinkle in the breeze.

Now it's time to bless your faery altar. Set out your food and beverage offerings, and light a stick of incense or drop some essential oil onto the ground. Sing or play beautiful music. Sprinkle a little bit of fine glitter over everything. Blow bubbles and enjoy the feeling of being in nature.

Once you have the fae's attention, speak softly to them. Tell them you believe in them and respect them. Let them know you'd be honored if they'd visit your altar from time to time, and that they can join in your rituals if they wish.

When you are ready to complete the blessing, take a deep breath and think a happy thought. It may take a few months before the fae accept your invitation, but have patience. If you believe in them, they'll believe in you too.

Astrea Taylor
Astrea Taylor is the author of *Belle Dame Sans Merci* and a practicing Witch. She resides in Dayton, Ohio.

The Roadside Shrine

In college I took a special course called Shrine Making (art school for the win!). We covered the history, spirituality, and design of altars, shrines, and other human-made sacred locations. One thing that stuck with me was the discussion on roadside shrines. As these are often associated with the outdoors, I wanted to finish this chapter by touching briefly on several kinds.

The first kind of roadside shrines are places that people make a pilgrimage to and then interact with in some way, usually as part of a larger religion and typically connected to a deity, saint, or spirit. These shrines could be temples, sacred stone markers, gravesites, churches, specially marked trees, wells, springs, statuary, etc. They are typically sites that have been traveled to for centuries—visited by thousands, if not millions, of people over a very long time. Their initial association with their related personality sparked their power, but this power is built on by every person who visits the site.

There are also modern marvels: roadside attractions. As Neil Gaiman talks about in his novel *American Gods*, tourist attractions have a certain power to them as well. Even if a location isn't tied to some classic myth or historical figure, roadside attractions start with the novelty of human invention and expand out from there. When people start coming to a place to spend their time (and their money), the site often gets a certain hum to it. We become curious because others were curious—we want to see it too. Time and money are the offerings we make. Then we take a souvenir with us to say we've been there. It's essentially an installation of performance art, completed by the onlooker. The House on the Rock in Wisconsin and the World's Largest Ball of Twine in Kansas may not seem like sacred sites, but they honor both human ingenuity and nature.

Lastly, there are the literal shrines along the edges of roads, marking where people have lost their lives in accidents or other tragedies. These especially stand out to me, because these crosses, flowers, stuffed animals, and other objects don't mark where the person was buried—clearly that was somewhere else. Rather, these shrines mark the departure point—the actual place (or very close to it) where these people unfortunately lost their lives. These shrines act as memorials to the deceased but also function as a warning to the living to remember that life is fragile, and we must cherish it while we can. This type of shrine is an altar to a lost life and a message to us all.

CHAPTER EIGHT

Altars for the Dead
(Tempest)

We can separate altars into three kinds: those that are for the divine (such as devotional shrines), those that are for the living (our seasonal and daily altars), and those that are for the dead (ancestral altars and altars for the recently deceased). This neatly sums up the mysteries of our world—why we live, how we live, and life after death. In this chapter we'll consider some of our practices concerning the latter, including the different kinds of altars we create to honor our dead.

Cemeteries and Grave Markers

We're not the only creatures that honor our dead on this planet, but we probably win the award for making the biggest show of it. The moment humanity started to honor the dead marked a new beginning in our mental thought processes. Archaeologists have uncovered ancient burial sites where the bodies were decorated with pigments, dressed in finery, accompanied by tools of the trade or beloved companions, and placed carefully and purposely within the earth. These sites give us glimpses into the burial practices of our ancestors, signifying that they found deep meaning in the change from life to death and also honored the personality that housed that body. These practices could have hinted at a belief in the afterlife, but it's also possible that we just didn't want to see the bodies of our loved ones eaten by bears and wolves. There are "air burials" in numerous cultures, where the body is left exposed to the elements and animals (particularly birds) in order to help the spirit depart and return the body to nature.

A gravestone not only marks the spot where someone has been buried but also gives the living a place to connect with the dead, to remember them and perform rituals to honor them. Tending to the gravesites of our loved ones can be an intimate and powerful experience. Many people use that time to "talk" with the dead, keeping them updated on what's happening in their lives and the rest of the family news. The act of placing fresh flowers, silk flower arrangements, or wreaths by a grave has multiple meanings as well. Flowers are a symbol of life and vitality, yet they are also fragile. There is also rich symbolic meaning behind flowers and their arrangements. The kinds and colors of flowers that are left at a gravesite may hint at the kind of relationship that exists between the living and their dead. Also, the seasonal changing out of flowers and wreaths can make us feel like we are still celebrating our holidays with those who have passed on.

Not only can we comfort ourselves by talking to the dead as we freshen flowers, weed, and clean stones by a grave, but we can also leave them mail. Some people see visiting a grave as a way to petition the dead for aid, which may be done in the form of notes, letters, or other small presents. I once was commissioned to paint a mailbox by the mother of a young man who had passed away tragically. The idea behind the mailbox was that his friends and family could leave letters for him. It was a way to alleviate their grief while also hoping to make sure his spirit rested in peace.

Another tradition I've experienced is the Jewish custom of leaving stones behind when you visit the deceased, which has a variety of meanings depending on who you ask. Some believe the rocks correspond to and acknowledge the brutality and hardships of life, while others say a rock symbolizes memory that never dies. Another custom I've seen across several cultures is leaving coins behind. Not only does the material they're made out of (metal) represent longevity and value, but

Gravestone with rock markers

the coins may also act as tokens for the dead to use on their next journey. In Chinese culture there is joss paper (aka spirit money) that is burned so the ancestors have spending money in the afterlife—the physical turned into the spiritual by fire.

In the last century in our society, we have unfortunately moved in a direction to push death and matters of death further and further away from us. Social customs have changed to separate the living from the dead, from the custom of holding a wake (with the deceased's body) inside the family home, to moving wakes to funeral parlors, to burying the dead in plots that are far away from where we live instead of in our backyards or down the street. This is unfortunate on so many levels, considering our society has also pushed hard to move the experience of birth outside of the home. We've become separated from experiencing the natural processes of both life and death in our homes. "Messy" as they can be, we lose important connections to who we are in the process. Thankfully there is a trend toward welcoming doulas back into modern culture, both the midwifery kind and those who handle matters of death and dying.

In most cases today, due to complicated laws, utility concerns, and health regulations, even if we own the land, we often can't be buried on it. Now, if someone has chosen to be cremated, it's pretty easy to keep them close by (if that was their wish, versus having their remains released into an ocean, sprinkled over a favorite garden, etc.). What if you really appreciate the graveside customs but your loved one is buried far away from you? You can still make space for them in or around your home in a multitude of ways. You can set up a place in your garden with a small stone marker, statue, or plant in their honor. You can create an indoor ancestral/family altar featuring photographs and objects that remind you of them. Or you can do a little bit of sympathetic magick, like I did for my grandparents.

My grandparents are buried across the country from where I live and almost two hours from where my parents live. I was able to attend my grandfather's funeral, and there was a tall pine tree near the grave. As a little girl, we would often take nature hikes together, where he would show me different kinds of seed pods, flowers, and other interesting bits of nature. As I recalled that during the ceremony, a pine cone came to rest by my feet. I picked it up, and it has traveled with me through several moves. It reminds me of him, and of where both of my grandparents now lay buried together. Similarly, you could weave together some blades of grass, press down flowers that may be growing nearby, or use any other natural elements that can be safely contained and preserved.

There are a multitude of magickal practices surrounding graveyard dirt (in Hoodoo, Voodoo, etc.). Some of these have to do with knowing the deceased, and the others are more concerned with the quality or personality of the deceased individual and various kinds of spellcraft. I'm not going to talk here about pressing a spirit of a loved one (or anyone else) into service, but I do believe that the fresh dirt from the grave of a loved one can be carried with us, and used to connect with them and honor them.

Grave Dirt, Grand Life: A Memory Spell

Let's say a loved one has passed on and you want to keep their spirit alive respectfully. You can't visit their gravesite because of distance, but you want to have a regular reminder of them that you can attend to. If you are able to take some dirt from their graveside with you, a potent thing you can do is to mix that soil with a potted plant that you know you will care for regularly. Ideally you want a kind of houseplant that is not an annual, so that it will stay alive (with proper care and attention). If you can't have indoor plants due to allergies, cats, or poor conditions, you could also consider burying the dirt next to a strong tree near you. You don't want to place the dirt in a vessel. It should be free to mingle with the environment around it, continuing on with the life cycle. As you mix the soil, you can say:

The dirt of your grave
Joins the dirt of life,
So in mind and heart
You'll be in my sight.

If you must move away from the outdoor site (I assume you'd take a potted plant with you or give it to another family member), simply take a new sample of the soil with you and repeat the ritual once you are settled.

LTAR-NATIVES

Cemeteries: The Altars of Our Ancestors

IT'S SEPTEMBER, MY Aunt Vinnie's birthday and the first time Mom and I are making the pilgrimage to visit her since she passed away last year. We've come prepared. I've packed a small bunch of red chrysanthemums (red was her favorite color), biscotti from an Italian bakery of which she approved (not everyone uses enough anisette), and a cup of espresso, piping hot. At the cemetery, my mother and I dust off the stone and place our offerings on it. I pour the espresso right into the ground. I keep an ancestor altar at home, but this,

Aunt Vinnie's last resting place, is a powerful place of honor and memory. If I close my eyes, I can recall the day of the funeral, and then the days, months, and years leading up to it. At this altar, the floodgates of the past open. What is remembered lives.

Say "ancestor altar" and inevitably thoughts turn to the *ofrenda* of Latin American tradition (though ofrendas are also cross-cultural and come in different shapes and forms). Not reserved exclusively for Dia de los Muertos celebrations, these altars are a constant presence in the homes of those who practice ancestor worship. Images or representations of the deceased, their favorite foods and objects, and sometimes money and flowers are laid out like a banquet—food for the spirit, and encouragement to stop and stay for a spell.

As much as I love cemeteries, I don't expect to spend much time in one when I pass from this life. But these places—part park and wildlife refuge, part art and history museum, and, of course, part genealogical record—are ancestor altars on a grand scale. The land is the base, and every flower and tree is magical. In every living thing is the presence of the four elements. Each tombstone is a magical talisman, and the cemetery gates and walls are delineators of sacred space. Zoom in and you'll see that a cemetery is a grand altar encompassing many smaller ones.

Altars for the Dead

Some gravestones are actually shaped like altars—table tombs at which the Mighty Dead can feast in the hereafter. Whether an upright headstone, a statue, or an obelisk, these memorials are altars. Besides the names, dates, and sometimes photos and pertinent and important symbols etched into their surfaces, there are earthly remains here—that carbon content that connects the lot of us. It's powerful stuff. And then there are the offerings.

Aunt Vinnie's is not the only grave I visit with gifts. Every December we place evergreens over my noni's headstone. At Aunt Jo's mausoleum, the glow of a tiny tealight on the floor finds its way up the wall of names to hers. The plot of my father's family has no stone; it's a blank green sea surrounded by islands of granite and marble. Here, I bring flowers and arrange them in a circle—sacred space in which to make a connection to those whose blood flows in my veins. Here, the earth is my altar, and the sacred lies beneath.

Go to the graveyard. Go prepared. Bring flowers. Bring candles and cakes. Bring beads and coins and coffee. Bring a token to leave as a reminder of your visit. Bring those things that your loved ones loved (and that are allowed—all cemeteries have rules for what can be left behind). Treat their last resting place as an altar, a sacred space of offering and devotion.

But what if you have no blood ancestors to visit? No dear ones?

You do. We, all of us, are part of the human family. Chances are you have some sort of connection to someone in just about any cemetery. I made the pilgrimage to Machpelah, a crumbling Victorian-era New York graveyard, to pay homage to Harry Houdini. His desperate desire to find proof of a life beyond this one was an aspect of his character that resonated strongly with me. Houdini—as far as I know—is no blood relation, and yet he is an ancestor. Inside the magic circle of his memorial there is a bust of the man himself and rows of pillow stones, each honoring a member of the Houdini family. In addition to the customary piles of stones (in Jewish cemeteries, to leave a stone is the mark of a visit), the master magician's grave is loaded with offerings: flowers, messages, coins, and cards (of the tarot variety—the Magician card mostly, of course). I've had similar experiences further afield. Countless nameless pilgrims leave beads and liquor and tobacco as offerings at the base of Marie Laveau's vault. I found guitar strings at Jimi Hendrix's grave, and rolled-up maps of Middle Earth planted around J.R.R. Tolkien's modest headstone, all altars to honor the dead.

Go to the cemetery. Speak aloud the names of those who have walked before, whether you know them personally or not. Are there graves that are lonely and untended? Clear them if you can. Leave an offering. Thank them for being. What is remembered lives.

Natalie Zaman

Natalie Zaman is the author of *Color and Conjure* and *Magical Destinations of the Northeast* (Llewellyn); the co-author of *Sirenz* (Flux), *Sirenz Back in Fashion* (Flux), and *Blonde Ops* (Thomas Dunne Books); and a contributor to various Llewellyn annuals.

Altars for the Deceased and the Ancestors (Jason)

Many Witches place a strong personal emphasis on working with the spirits of those they have lost and honoring their ancestors, both immediate and those further up the family tree. At Samhain most years I build an altar just for my grandparents so that I can honor them and remind their spirits that I'm thinking of them both. Those altars to my grandparents contain their pictures and things they owned in their lifetime, including a few lovely letters written by my grandmother to my grandfather while he was serving in World War II.

Because my grandparents were Christians, I don't adorn their altar with much in the way of Pagan or witchy stuff. Instead, I focus on things they owned, their images, and things they liked in their lifetime. My gramps enjoyed his whisky, so placing a good bottle of single malt on the altar seems like a fine way to attract his spirit. The old magickal adage "Like attracts like" applies to devotional altars and altars to both gods and ancestors.

Though it's not quite an altar, we have a shrine to the Mighty Dead of the Craft in our ritual space. It's not nearly as elaborate as the altar to my grandparents, but it serves as a place to thank those folks for their contributions to the Craft. Every October we induct more of the Mighty Dead into that shrine, giving those spirits an open invitation to visit our rites whenever they wish.

It's possible to make an altar to ancestors both known and unknown. If you know your family's history, you may want to honor that history by including things about the culture(s) those ancestors grew up in. Place things representing that culture's food and heritage upon your altar in order to make those spirits feel welcome. These things don't have to be elaborate, just welcoming. Be sure the spirits feel invited.

Summoning the Spirits with the Altar Pentacle (Jason)

Because of its ability to act as a conduit between the world of spirit and that of the living, the pentacle is an ideal place to reconnect with the souls of those who have been lost to us. There are many ways within Witchcraft to connect to the Summerlands, but the pentacle is one of the easier ways and one of the most practical.

If you are performing this rite alone, it's not necessary to do a full ritual setup before beginning, but I do suggest at least casting a circle and calling upon the Lord and Lady (and/or specific deities associated with the dead, such as Persephone, Hades, Cernunnos, or Hella). You'll also need to round up a candle and at least a picture of the deceased individual you'd like to contact or an object that once belonged to them. The more pictures and objects you can gather up, the better. If you don't have a picture or object, you can write the person's name on a piece of paper and use that.

Start by placing the candle on your pentacle. If your pentacle is small, you can place the candle near the top of your pentacle, right above the single point of the star. Once the candle is positioned properly, light it while saying:

I light this candle to serve as a light in the darkness and a beacon to welcome back one who has been lost to me. May its light guide those I have loved and lost to this place, and may its power chase away any spirit that is not welcome in this place and would do me harm. So mote it be!

Then place the pictures/items of the one you are trying to contact on the pentacle. If you have numerous items and they won't all fit on the pentacle, just set them around it. This is an important step, because in the world of magick like attracts like. The more objects/pictures you have that reference or belonged to the deceased, the better your chances of success. Once the items have been arranged, draw an invoking pentagram above your pentacle and the candle upon (or above) it.

While drawing the pentagram, state your intentions:

Tonight I open this door to the realm of spirit. I seek reunion with (name of the person you are calling), who has been lost to me in this world. With love and light let them return to this place so that I might remember their touch, their voice, and their heart. Let them hear my words and feel my emotions as we reunite and experience each other once more. The door is open. If they will it, may they come to this space and be welcome in it. So mote it be!

If you are calling upon the deceased simply to experience their presence, this is the time to do that. Open up all of your senses and listen and feel for any sign from the spirit you have summoned. Sometimes I find that they are easier to reach if I close my eyes and meditate upon them at this part in the ritual. Spirits of the deceased do not interact with us like they did while in the world of the living, but I truly believe that we can feel their power and their presence near us. How we experience those things often serves as a way to convey messages to us in this world.

If you are calling someone for a specific purpose, you should state that at this time. I often call upon the spirit of my grandmother for advice, and when I do so I usually say something like this:

Grandmother, I seek your soul this night because I wish for your counsel. When you were with me in this world, your wisdom and advice were always a great help to me. I am now dealing with a problem and I need that advice once more. There are individuals saying things about me that are not true. How can I overcome this? How can I get them to stop? Any insight you can offer me would be welcome.

Here again I close myself off and concentrate on my surroundings, and reach out for a sign from the spirit. When addressing my grandmother, I often hear her voice near my ear, but not always. Sometimes there's a slight stirring of the wind that brings to mind a good hug, and in other instances I feel enveloped by a comforting energy that reminds me of her. Again, just how the dead contact each of us is highly variable.

There have also been times when I've gotten no answer and all. When that happens, I often redraw my invoking pentagram one or two times and then chant the name of the soul I'm reaching out to. If that doesn't work, I just close up the circle and revisit the problem another day. Even those dead whom we are closest to sometimes have other things to do away from us, so don't get discouraged if you don't get the results you are looking for.

When you do get an answer, be sure to thank the spirit who visited. If you believe in giving gifts to the dead (see chapter 6 on devotional altars), this would be a good time to do that. End your rite by drawing a banishing pentagram over the pentacle and candle while saying:

(Name of person who visited), thank you for joining me in this rite. As our time together is now at an end, I wish you a safe journey back to your realm. You are gone from this world but will never be forgotten. All will be as it once was, and this window shall now be closed. So mote it be!

Banishing Pentacle

End the rite by blowing out your candle, thanking the gods, and taking down your circle. If you left the spirit you summoned a gift, remove it from your altar and give it to the Earth when the time is right.

ALTAR-NATIVES

*Ancestor Altar: Enveloping
All My Family Members*

I GREW UP in a matriarchal family, with family members who loved to tell stories over and over, so my ancestors were as real to me as the living ones I knew. My parents divorced when I was five, and my dad disappeared, never to be seen again. I knew he was Portuguese and was born in Hawaii before it was a state, but that couldn't hold a candle to my knowledge of my German/Austrian maternal side of the family. We had stories, events, much drama, history, and laughter.

Fast-forward to decades later, when I found myself in Asheville, North Carolina. I spent much time in the local Witch store, the delightful Raven & Crone, and soon heard about ancestor altars, just as the leaves began to turn to their jewel-toned colors. An ancestor altar? What exactly was that? The store had a lovely reverential altar filled with candles, statues, the names of the deceased, and more. Could I do the same? As I am wont to do, I did some research, and soon came up with what is now my own ancestor altar.

The first year, I had the basics: candles and black-and-white photos of my parents' glamorous wedding, my beloved oma (grandmother), and some aunts and uncles. It felt good to honor my parents especially, as they had shown up strongly when I moved to Asheville—mostly my mother, who could not resist telling me what to do with my life. Some things never change, and with the veil so thin, she took advantage of it. My dad would show up on occasion. I was slower to listen to him, although he had been sending me messages persistently over the years. *Remember my side of the family*, he would tell me. *Don't forget us*, his mom would convey, offering a Hawaiian orchid as a sign of her presence.

Altars for the Dead

The next year, I dug deep. One of my most treasured possessions is a photo album my mother compiled, full of pictures of her life, married life, and our family life. It stopped right when my parents divorced, so it's a treasure trove of history a bit before my time, mixed with a few baby and toddler photos of me. I found photos of my dad's relatives, including his mother. I added them to my ancestor altar, along with a few items that reminded me of them. I felt the knot of my family anguish untying as I gazed upon my wonderfully eclectic and dynamic family. I cried a bit, seeing for the first time the entire scope of my family. I am the proud daughter of two very distinct lineages, and at that moment, I hoped they were proud of me. I had never really thought of them all together like that before. It had always been "us" and "them." For the first time, we were all together: a mini family reunion via an ancestor altar. I remain thankful.

Lisa Wagoner

Lisa Wagoner is a freelance writer, poet, and independent scholar, as well as a Priestess at Mother Grove Goddess Temple in Asheville, North Carolina. She follows Brigid and is an eclectic Pagan.

LTAR-NATIVES

Chinese Altars for Ancestors

CHINESE ANCESTOR WORSHIP practices can vary. There are the base traditions, and then religious angles thrown in on top, usually Buddhist or Christian. The process begins at the gravesite, where feng shui dictates the location of a grave in order to provide a respectful place of rest for the deceased. Whenever possible, the dead are buried on a hillside with their feet facing downhill, ideally with a waterfront or otherwise good view. The idea is that this arrangement resembles an armchair that is supported in the back and made to be as comfortable as possible, as historically only the elite could afford armchairs. (This holds true for the living as well.) By doing this, the hope is that the deceased will be placated and bring their descendants good luck, health, and prosperity. Just about everything in Chinese culture is about these three things—and food.

On a personal level, you're more likely to find altars among the Buddhists or those who are holding on to tradition. On these altars a variety of items can be found, such as pictures/name tablets of the deceased, incense, a dish (typically with three tangerines; the Chinese word for *tangerine* is a homonym of the word for *gold*, symbolizing prosperity, and the word for *three* is a homonym of the word for *growth*), and the three gods ever together, Fuk Luk Sau (Cantonese pronunciation: *Fuk* and *Luk* rhyme with *book*, and *Sau* with *sow*), representing good luck, prosperity, and longevity.

The altar is placed somewhere high, like on a dresser or bookshelf (shopkeepers attach them high up on walls facing doorways) in a prominent part of the house that isn't the kitchen, bedroom, or bathroom. Some use a small red and gold altar (symbolizing good luck and prosperity, respectively, and also armchair-shaped) to contain everything. In Christian immigrant households such as my immediate and extended family, you have a greater chance of at least seeing the trio of gods, who aren't so much worshiped as kept out of respect for tradition.

For active worship, there are cycles throughout the month where relatives will light incense and offer food to their ancestors at their home altar. For the recently deceased, prayers and burned-paper versions of material goods (money, microwaves, cars, etc.) are offered during the first seven days, to ensure a good future for all. Outside the home, regardless of religion, there are two annual festivals to visit gravesites.

Ching Ming (meaning "clean/bright"), the festival that falls on either April 4 or 5, is when families go and tidy up family gravesites and leave offerings. The second festival is Chung Yeung, on the ninth day of the ninth lunar month, and is the last chance to clean up the gravesites and leave offerings before winter. Offerings for both festivals can range from flowers to food and incense. Around these dates you'll find traditional foods for sale for both the living and the dead that are not normally available the rest of the year, such as different types of steamed paste cakes and dumplings.

Jade
Jade is an artist and designer residing in the Pacific Northwest.

CHAPTER NINE

Altars on the Go
(Tempest)

Sometimes having a permanent setup for your altar isn't the way to go. Maybe you spend a lot of time on the road traveling or have to relocate quite often for work or other reasons. Perhaps your housing situation isn't ideal for you to display your altar out in the open. So it would make more sense to focus your energy on having a portable altar that's easy to take with you or one that's discreet or hidden.

To make a traveling or portable altar, consider what you need to take with you. What are your size limits, climate concerns, and travel restrictions? What's the purpose of your altar? Are you carrying an image of a deity, spirit, or saint along with you? Are you doing a meditation practice that includes burning incense or candles? Are you anointing yourself with an oil? Does your altar have an elemental focus? Is it a memory box or an anchor for your home base?

Does the altar need to fit in your pocket or purse, or is it something that will live in a suitcase? If you're traveling by plane, will it be checked luggage or a carry-on? If a carry-on, will it clear TSA? Liquids and gels currently must be 3.4 ounces or less, and be sure to stay away from anything sharp or that looks like a weapon.

Consider climate concerns. Are you going somewhere humid? Very hot or very cold? It doesn't take a lot of heat to start melting wax, especially when inside a metal container. (I discovered this with ChapStick while camping at Pagan Spirit Gathering.)

Tiny Wonders

Don't underestimate the power of small altars! Just because a sacred space is little doesn't mean it is ineffective. In fact, diminutive altars can help strengthen your practice with their intimate nature, as well as help hold secrets in the palm of your hand.

Matchboxes and Mint Tins

I have seen many matchbox altars over the years, and most of them tend to land in the realm of folk art, versus actual altars you would carry with you. They are typically delicate works of art meant to be placed on a shelf, in a tiny nook, etc. It makes sense when you consider that the majority of matchboxes are just thin cardboard—meant to be temporary, since they contain items that are meant to be burned up. So an actual matchbox (unless it's one of those rare fancy ones made of wood) isn't ideal for something you want to travel with. Though if you are looking to make a tiny biodegradable altar for a specific occasion, then a matchbox is a pretty good idea. On the other hand, the metal containers that some cough drops, mints, and candies come in can make a really durable little travel altar.

Cigar Boxes, Shoe Boxes, Cash Boxes, and Other Caches

Once you get a bit bigger with these kinds of boxes, you're getting a combination storage box/physical altar in the form of a small platform. Cigar boxes are wonderful because they're often made of excellent wood and can be fragrant as well as decorative. Shoeboxes are made of cardboard, so they're not as durable as wood, but they are lightweight and *very* unassuming on the outside (unless you happen to have a box for some expensive brand of shoes). The upside of having a cash box altar is that it is often watertight and durable and has a built-in lock. The downside of hiding your altar in a cash box is that it may be the first thing someone tries to steal.

LTAR-NATIVES

Making a Traveling Protection Altar

AN ALTAR DOESN'T have to sit in just one spot. Travel altars are portable enough to assemble when you get where you are going, simple enough to take apart, and small enough to store easily. A travel altar can be carried in a pocket-size container, always ready for magic and just a glovebox or purse away. No matter the style, a travel altar makes magic on the road easy. For this project you will need:

An empty mint tin

A hot glue gun and hot glue sticks

A small piece of black fabric, slightly larger than your tin

A small printed image of your patron/patroness (Or, if you aren't sure which deity to use, try an image of Saint Michael.)

A small black tourmaline stone

A small hematite stone

To begin, use your hot glue gun to affix the fabric to the inside of the mint tin. You can choose to make it tight against the walls of the container or a little looser so the fabric appears to be billowy. Use your artistic eye and let this process be fun. Allow the glue to set, then affix your chosen image to the center of the fabric against what would be the bottom of the tin. Ideally, this image will look like it is framed by the black fabric when you stand the mint tin on its side. Finally, use your hot glue to affix the tourmaline and hematite stones to either side of your image along the sides of the tin. So when you stand the mint tin up on its side, these two stones will be along the bottom. As you create your protection altar, chant the word *protection* to help charge your intention.

When completed, you can put the altar in your car or your purse or take it along with you when going out of town. Now you've got a simple yet powerful travel altar for protection and safety.

Phoenix LeFae
**Phoenix LeFae is the author of *Hoodoo Shrines and Altars*.
She is a Gardnerian and an initiate in the Reclaiming
Tradition of Witchcraft and the Avalon Druid Order.
Find out more about her and her metaphysical shop, Milk
& Honey, at www.Milk-and-Honey.com.**

Paper Altars

Sometimes you just need to go absolutely two-dimensional to have a travel or hidden altar. All you need for a paper altar is—you guessed it—a piece of paper. It could be the size of a business card, an index card, or a regular sheet that you can fold up and place in your wallet, pocket, or book. You can print or glue images of deities on it, or simply draw symbols or write words. Paper altars are wonderful because they take up barely any space and are relatively invisible when tucked away, and best of all, you can hold them in your hands.

One possible layout would be to mark the four directions with *N E S W*, and use a symbol for each element (alchemical or more pictorial). Then place a pentacle in the center, with the name or names of deities you align with around it. You could also laminate your paper altar (easy to do at most copy/print shops) so it's durable. Sure, it's "just" paper, but it's still a physical and very portable reminder of your practice. Your brain is your most powerful tool!

Altars for Vehicles

The dashboard seems to be the most common place to build an altar in a car, which makes sense because you can easily see it while driving. Another option is the back window shelf (if you have a sedan type of car versus a van or hatchback). Less common is using the center console (usually where the change goes and drink holders live), as well as the floor of the passenger side (which is a nice place to put symbols for spirits that you bring with you—as long as you leave enough foot room for physical passengers!). I've also seen tiny altars within the windshields of motorcycles, so where there's a will, there's a way!

Not surprisingly, the most common items found on dashboard altars often have to do with safety, speed, and protection with regard to travel. The Hindu god Ganesha, with his elephant head, is known for removing obstacles. Other people prefer Hermes, with his winged feet. Catholics tend to favor the Virgin Mary and also Saint Christopher, the patron saint of travelers. I've even seen statues featuring variations of the deity we call Squat, the goddess of parking spots. *(Squat, Squat, find us a spot!)*

Items that hang from the rearview mirror tend to be tasseled, sparkly, or mirrored—which harkens back to classic items used to ward off the evil eye (and, in this case, probably the eyes of the parking enforcement and speed-trap cops). It is said that tassels, beads, mirrors, patterns, and items that create movement confuse and fascinate evil spirits, so their attention goes elsewhere. Fuzzy dice or playing cards, on the other hand, could be seen as tempting Fate or courting Fortuna or Lady Luck. There are also natural items such as rocks, shells, twigs, and flowers that we may collect on travels, taking a small piece of the spirit of that place with us. I especially like to collect fragrant items such as sage, roses, and lavender while I'm on the road, as they not only look beautiful but also make the car smell wonderful. I then place them on our outdoor shrine once we get back home. (Make sure that any items you hang from the rearview mirror don't block your view of the road.)

If you wish to adhere things to your dash or other hard surfaces of the car, there are an array of methods you can use. Some folks swear by blue gummy adhesive putty or Quake-HOLD! putty. I've seen others use Velcro with adhesive—that way, you can easily remove items and reattach them. Both these methods are somewhat better than using double-sided tape, duct tape, or gaffer tape. Sure, those will hold, but they get messy quickly. If you live someplace where your vehicle will cook once it gets warmer, you'll have to replace the adhesive material regularly. All of these products can be cleaned up with a degreaser and elbow grease, though they may ruin the finish.

As someone who lives in the city and travels a lot, I caution you not to make your vehicle altar too elaborate or shiny, unless you have a great alarm system or live out in the middle of nowhere. You don't want to attract the eyes of thieves or the ire of close-minded people who think vandalism can be an act of their god. Also, be sure not to make your altar something that could easily come loose and injure you or a passenger or distract you and cause an accident. Attach that stuff securely, and don't use anything that could be a dangerous projectile!

Dashboard altar

If you like the idea of having an altar for your vehicle but you want to keep it on the down low, consider putting what you need in a small satchel that you can hang from the rear-view mirror (if that's legal in your area—in some places it's not!) or keep in the glovebox or somewhere else relatively hidden but handy.

Taking the Indoor Altar Outdoors and On the Road

There are altars that travel with us and there are altars that travel only on occasion. Sometimes all this means is that an

261
· · ·
Altars on the Go

indoor altar is brought outdoors temporarily—for a personal ritual or a gathering or other event. For a brief time, a folding table, picnic bench, or blanket can become the base of an altar and the focus of a ritual.

Whether you are going a short distance, such as from your living room to your backyard, or a long distance, like a car or plane ride to a convention, there are some important things to consider.

When making the seemingly simple switch from inside to outside altar, there are some key things to consider: How level is the ground for your altar furniture? How will the wind affect candles, cloths, and offerings? Will bugs or animals cause complications? Outside is generally not the place for lightweight candleholders, delicate statues, or fragile glassware. Even if the weather seems calm, it's better to be safe than sorry. Weight down any tablecloths, use sturdy vases and holders, don't leave food or drink exposed prior to the ritual, and watch for potential fire hazards. You may also need a heavy-duty lighter to set things aflame.

When it's a short trip, we typically hand-carry things outside, one at a time, carefully. But even then, I find it can be a very good idea to wrap items up in towels or blankets and lay them down on the ground until you are ready. The wind or the neighbor's dog could easily knock something over while you're in between trips. It's best to wait until you've got everything collected outside before assembling the altar.

If you're getting in a vehicle, it's wise to take some precautions. Again, towels, blankets, and pillowcases make great insulation for delicate items. For added security, place fragile statues (once they are wrapped up in fabric) in a larger plastic bin. These can be found for cheap, with lids, at any big-box or craft store. Place heavy items on the bottom and more fragile items on top. Don't overpack it! You may want to line the bin first with more fabric or lightweight pillows. You can also use newspaper, but be careful with items with light-colored surfaces, such as resin and marble, as the printing may rub off on them. Also, you won't have to go chasing down wayward fabric on a windy day at the park. Fabric stays put—paper wants to see you run. Also, fabric can double as an altar cloth!

If you want to win the award for the most effective, fanciest traveling Witch, you could have a beautiful sturdy box that doubles as a container *and* an altar. Just remember, wood weighs more than plastic, so don't make or get a box that's too heavy for you to easily carry or hold once everything is in it.

Virtual and Digital Altars

Last but not least, we have the ultimate stealth altar: the digital one—and the ones that exist only in cyberspace. Considering that many of us spend a fair amount of time on our computers, tablets, and phones, it makes a lot of sense to use their screens as altars. They are tools of communication, and we can easily change and collect images to view on them, plus add a soundtrack! You can change your desktop image to focus on a particular deity or spirit whenever you wish. Another way to have an interactive, virtual devotional altar is to create a webpage dedicated to whatever spirit or deity you honor. With the wealth of social media websites and free, easy-to-use software available, it's easy to create a Tumblr, Instagram, or Facebook page or a Wix site where you collect images, music, poems, and stories all related to a deity or element. By regularly visiting the site and adding to it, you are keeping it active. It's also a great way to communicate with others who have similar beliefs or dedications.

LTAR-NATIVES

Altar Tools and the All-Powerful Smartphone

WHILE MANY PEOPLE prefer ritual tools that harken back to the eighteenth century, including candles, herbs, oils, and other such things, technological devices are often powerful aids to magical and theurgical ceremonies. Currently, smartphones and tablets are ubiquitous and powerful methods of communication. Although many people do not conceptualize the smartphone as a magical device, we can think of it as a Vulcan-blessed tool of mercurial goodness (or, if you have checked social media lately, perhaps not-goodness). To start, a smartphone with Spotify/Apple Music/Google Music/Amazon and a pair of headphones or a speaker can provide music to enhance the mood of any ritual. Meditation timers can guide you gently in and out of meditation practice. Products like the Hue system or other LED lighting systems allow you to use special bulbs to create environments with colored projected light, giving you the ability to add color for chakra work, planetary colors, or any other correspondence you might want to use.

These tools allow you to change your ritual setup easily, and you do not have to buy fabric or paint that you might use only once or twice. Controlling the environment in this manner is a relatively safe way to increase the mood and effectiveness of your rituals with little preparation using only your phone or tablet.

We can use these devices in other ways too. Are you summoning a spirit or doing a conjure-style spell where you need a picture of a person you are doing some healing work for but you can't or don't want to print it out? Use the image on your smartphone as your focal point. Celebrating a goddess? Pull up a painting/representation of her on your tablet or phone and use a micro projector to display it on the wall.

To use a phone or computer in this way does require a bit of machine empathy. After all, electronics tend to burn out around magical energies. Have you ever seriously blessed your cell phone? If you are using methods from my book *Hands-On Chaos Magic*, making a servitor out of your smartphone, tablet, or computer allows you to feed energy into it so it can protect itself and harden the tool to be more resilient so you can use it to act as a direct conduit for magical energies. Most religions have a god/spirit of technology that, if petitioned, will gladly harden your technology to handle magical energies. (Being initiated into Vodou, I often pray to Ogun.) If you spend some time doing this with your devices, they will also tend to function better and last longer.

Once your tool has been hardened by the various forces, you can ask other gods and goddesses to apply other energies to it. Need to communicate more effectively? Charge your device with mercurial energy. Need to communicate more compassionately? Charge your device with Venusian energy and then use this in ritual. Your imagination is the only limit.

While most people do not think of a cell phone, tablet, or laptop as a magical tool, in a pinch it can be the only thing you need in order to do very effective magick. With a charged and blessed piece of technology, you will never be stuck in a hotel room needing to do some sort of magic and lacking your tools. In addition, so much of the modern world relies on technology, so why not incorporate some tech into your altars?

Andrieh Vitimus

Andrieh Vitimus is the author of the modern magical classic *Hands-On Chaos Magic: Reality Manipulation Through the Ovayki Current*. Andrieh motivates, facilitates, and captivates with his workshops across the world in coaching, business, and the occult.

CHAPTER
TEN

Troubleshooting an Altar
(Tempest & Jason)

There are some commonsense things you should consider when designing your altar. For example, thinking about fire and its effects ahead of time is a must. If you plan to burn a lot of candles, make sure the altar is as fireproof as possible—from the surface it's on to what's above it, and anything else that could get in the way. An altar on a shelf with fabric curtains is a really neat idea, but there's too great a fire risk if you plan on working with votives and tapers and burning things in your cauldron. Another thing to think about is food. If you want to make offerings of food that won't get moldy or attract bugs indoors, then you'll want to either build your altar outside or keep those offerings on a plate or bowl that's easy to transport outside to disperse to the plants, birds, and other animals without causing issues.

But what about the more unusual things you may encounter on your journey? Throughout this book we've covered a lot of crucial ways to prevent or at least minimize mishaps and accidents from happening at or with your altar. But we figured most people would find it very helpful to have some frequently asked questions addressed in one easy section. We asked our friends and our online acquaintances about the most common issues they've faced, and there was indeed an overlap. From dealing with disturbances and metaphysical dilemmas to figuring out how to protect, respect, clean, and refresh your altar, we've got you covered.

Dealing with Others
How do you cat-proof an altar, or protect one that isn't cat-proof?

JM: You can keep all of your athames and white-handled knives pointing upward so that when your cat jumps on the altar … This is a real problem and there's no easy answer here. Until this past Saturday night, I didn't believe that my cats ever played on our primary working altar, but I caught one of them red-pawed. My cry of "You terrible beast!" was probably not enough to completely dissuade them from ever repeating their little act.

There are mundane solutions, such as sprays with scents that cats don't like that keep them away from things. And as Witches, there's always magick! A quick spell to keep the cat away from the top of your altar might be advisable, such as "Cat, cat, go away! Find another place to play!"

Cat on altar

LTZ: You can try to "train" your cats by verbally emphasizing *NO* or maybe using a spray bottle to deter them if that has worked for you with other things, but you know that cat is going to be back on your altar as soon as you turn around. The best thing you can do is to make peace with it and don't put easily knocked-over and fragile items on altars that cats have access to. You could also make a separate altar for Bast and ask for her guidance and supervision. It might work. Might.

How do I stop or prevent other people from messing with my altar?

JM: You probably can't, unfortunately. Most Witches and Pagans are extremely well versed in Witch etiquette, the first rule of which is "keep your hands off my stuff." I think I've only ever had one fellow Pagan manhandle my altar, though getting her energy off my stuff took far longer than I wanted it to. Though not aesthetically pleasing, a sign would probably work, especially if you are throwing a party with a lot of non-magickal people present.

LTZ: Besides not making your altar easily visible or accessible to people you don't want to touch it, you can be upfront about house rules: "Please do not touch anything on the altar, under penalty of hex."

If things get damaged (by accident or through malice), what should be done with the broken items and how do I make amends to the gods?

JM: I bury my broken items, unless they are made of natural materials, such as wood, and in those cases I burn them in a ritual fire. I don't think there's any need to make amends with the gods for such things. They understand our limitations. We are human and are therefore imperfect. As long as the harm was unintentional, it should be fine. Now, if the damage was done maliciously, like you get mad at Thor and decide to break a statue of him, you should probably get ready for a shitstorm. The gods don't care for that kind of disrespect.

LTZ: I think the gods are generally understanding about mishaps and accidents, especially if they weren't intentionally caused by you. Now, in the case of someone else being a jerk, that's on them. For things that are broken and are repairable, I do what I can, bless them, then return them to the altar. If it's beyond hope, I sigh heavily and dispose of it properly.

Who can use an altar?

JM: The easy answer is "anyone," while the longer answer is probably "anyone who comes to the altar with the best of intentions."

LTZ: Yep. As long as their intent is sincere, then all is good.

Cleaning and Maintenance
How often should I clean my altar? Is dust on an altar okay, or is it offensive?

JM: I'll start by saying that dust on an altar is completely offensive, unless uncleanliness is a choice you've made your entire life. When we place a deity or a tool (such as the athame) that represents our true will on an altar, we are saying that those objects and ideas are important to us—and we take care of the things that are important to us.

I'll admit though that I can be a bit negligent about cleaning up my own altar, and there's no way around this really unless you put yourself on some sort of schedule. Because I use my altars regularly, I am paying attention to them, so nothing ever gets too bad. After a long day of working or whatever, cleaning up our altar space isn't always high on the priority list. But if we are dedicated Witches, we can find the time to do these things.

LTZ: Taking care of your altar should be part of a regular regimen. If you have difficulty regularly attending to your altar, creating a weekly cleaning schedule is a good way to solve that problem. Set a time and day, and keep to it. If you'll be away, then set a time for yourself when you get back. There are some situations where dust and cobwebs are considered both atmospheric and appropriate for certain deities and spirits, but those are few and far between.

What's the best way to keep an altar clean, tidy, and uncluttered?

JM: If something doesn't serve your altar, it should be removed. That's my first cardinal rule. Everything on your altar should mean something to you or the deities that are a part of it. That keeps a lot of extraneous stuff from ending up on my altars. Having several altars also helps keep things uncluttered. I know that not everyone has room for seven altars in their home, but if you can find the space, it makes a huge difference. (My house is not big either, but the tops of bookshelves are perfect for altars!)

LTZ: Really, what is uncluttered? That could be a design preference, but in general, ask yourself how workable your altar is. You should be able to do what you need to do without accidentally setting stuff on fire, spilling things, or knocking over important items. Also, be sure to remove offerings, finished spells, and other things once they have been used so they don't get in the way.

What's the best way to clean up spilled wax and wine?

LTZ: When you spill wax on fabric, get some newspaper and an iron. Remove as much excess wax as you can without damaging the fabric. Put the iron on the appropriate setting for the fabric. Put the newspaper on top, then move the iron around, heating up the wax. The newspaper will soak up the wax. You may need a *lot* of newspaper, depending on the size of the spill. Be careful not to get the iron covered in the wax. For spills on harder surfaces, some people swear by scraping up the wax with a credit card. You could also try using a hair dryer to heat up the wax, then soak it up with paper towels or newspaper. For wine, especially if it's red, it may be time for a new area rug! Clean it up as quickly as possible. Also, coasters are your friends.

JM: Tempest is on point with how to deal with wax, though sometimes I'll just pick at it until I get most of it out. We've spilled some wine over the years, but thankfully most of our altar cloths are red, so no one notices. If I get wax on a physical object, I'll throw that candleholder (or whatever it is) in the freezer for a night and the wax will generally break off pretty easily the next day. Our editor reminded us that club soda is a common remedy for wine stains (especially among Hungarians), and that salt poured over a spill will absorb a lot of the wine.

Alternatively, we could all switch to cakes and vodka during ritual, since vodka is clear and doesn't stain.

What can I do if I find myself out of or low on an altar supply that I consider essential (candles, incense, etc.)?

JM: There's always a work-around if you are out of something or running low on a particular thing. We don't *need* candles or incense to do a ritual or a working. They are simply nice to have. Don't have a candle and need a focus? You could always use the flashlight on your cell phone, or a candle gif (it'll even flicker and won't burn your hair). I know that sounds completely unmagickal, but we do what we have to do. I've got a kitchen full of herbs if I really find myself needing incense and I'm out of what I usually use. Magick and ritual are about *intent*, not the objects we use.

LTZ: MacGyver that stuff—be creative. There are other ways to work at your altar, so don't use that as an excuse. Also, add the item to your shopping list while you are thinking about it.

Objects and Design
What should I do with items that I no longer want on my altar?

JM: I try to give things away if they are still in working order. There's almost always a coven member who needs an extra tool or whatever else might have found its way onto my altar. If it's something really special that I don't want to give away and can't quite use anymore, then it gets buried or burned or is thrown into the ocean. (I realize how horrible this sounds, but I swear I'm not littering.)

LTZ: If it's something that's still useful, you can cleanse it and put it away for later, or pass it along to someone else if you don't need or want it anymore. If it's something that can't be reused, then if it makes you feel better, cleanse it before disposing of it properly. Fire can be fun (if the item is safe to burn!).

How do I safely introduce new items to my altar?

JM: Everything on your altar should resonate with your energies, so before putting that new thing on your altar, be sure to get a little bit of you on it first. Sometimes this can be as simple as finding a new tool and just picking it up and holding it for a while. Our things are sometimes drawn to us, and when that's the case, they fit with us as snugly as jigsaw puzzle pieces and it's not really an issue.

If it's something you are really worried about (I love this thing, but it feels icky to me!), you could bury it for a cycle of the moon and let the earth take away the negative energies that are a part of it. If you go this route, bury your object at the full moon and then retrieve it twenty-eight days later.

LTZ: Hey, altar! Look, I brought you a new friend! Seriously, if you felt drawn to acquire something of a sacred nature, it probably makes sense to place it on your altar. If you like a thing but get a feeling it doesn't belong on your altar, then consider another location for it. It might need its own altar. Add responsibly, and trust your gut.

Do I have to keep certain tools in specific locations?

JM: I think it's traditional in some paths to keep anything relating to the Goddess on one side of the altar and anything relating to the God on the other. This is only a good idea if it makes sense to you.

In the two covens my wife and I are a part of, our altar layout is the same for every ritual. My athame goes in one spot, the cup in another, etc. But part of that is because having everything in the same spot over and over again makes it easy to grab stuff in ritual. I know where the wand will be every time we do something. We are also big fans of tradition, and I find that setting up our working altar in the same way every time puts me in the mood for ritual.

LTZ: Nope. (At least not in the path that I follow.) Put your tools in locations that make them safe, accessible, and easy to use.

Is it best to have a symmetrical or an asymmetrical altar? An ornate or a minimal one?

JM: There's a big candle in the middle of our altar that's representative of spirit, and we see spirit as the uniting force that holds the universe together. So for me it makes sense that such a force would be in the center of everything, with all of our other tools radiating out from it. I'm also a big fan of order, so everything on my altar is balanced. If the Goddess statue is on the left side of the altar, the God statue is on the right in a similar spot.

Because I have many altars, some of them are ornate and some are minimal. The altar my coven uses in ritual is very minimal and only contains our working tools, some candles, and things representing the deities we are calling to in that particular ritual. My seasonal altars are rather ornate, with lots of stuff on them, as are my altars to specific deities. It all depends on the situation and what feels right to the individual Witch.

LTZ: I think it comes down to your personal preference and sense of order—as well as what the altar is supposed to do. I'm more likely to design an asymmetrical altar, because I find it more visually interesting and I rarely do or have things in pairs or sets. Technically it's still *balanced*, even though things aren't exactly even or split into even sections. Some people prefer a very minimal setup, one that is extremely clean and orderly, with a lot of space. Other people love the look and feel of lush, layered altars. I believe the overall feel of the altar is important, but it shouldn't be so overwhelming that it feels oppressive or so sparse that it looks like a sad Charlie Brown Christmas altar. The main concern is, does it work for your needs?

Harmony

Is it possible to have too many deities on my altar?

JM: I think so, because not every deity likes every other deity. And as a Witch who likes order, I only put compatible deities next to each other. Shiva does not need to share a space with Kokopelli, since they are worshiped in different ways in completely different parts of the world.

LTZ: I have yet to get to that point. If you're running out of room, then making a new altar may be required, if possible. But remember, it's not a game of whoever collects the most gods wins.

I think my deities don't like each other. What should I do?

JM: Find them separate rooms. Seriously, some deities do not play well with others. Santa Muerte, for instance, is a jealous goddess who mostly wants her own space. She doesn't want to be with Olympians or the denizens of Asgard (but she does get along with the loa of Voodoo and the orishas of Santeria). I'm friends with people who don't all like each other, so why should it be any different with the gods?

LTZ: If you can give them separate corners, altars, spaces, etc., that would be ideal. Otherwise it might be worth it to have a spiritual conference call, outlining boundaries and expectations.

How do I handle having altars dedicated to gods and ancestors in a single-room space and maintain my privacy and respect for them? (That is, do they really need to be peeking in on my…intimate moments?)

JM: I only invite gods and ancestors into my space who are respectful of my privacy.

LTZ: What's to stop them from doing that when your altar isn't in your bedroom? It's probably best not to think about that too much. Besides, you get to do it too once you're dead.

Santa Muerte altar

When and how do I decommission an altar for a deity I no longer work with?

JM: When I was a Witchling, I still had a bit of a Jesus hang-up, so I built him an altar. It felt like a good way to connect with my past and the members of my family who were still Christians. After several years it just didn't work for me anymore. I had no problem with Jesus (though some of his followers were a different story), but he wasn't really a part of my life anymore, and I just felt silly giving him altar space. It was time to decommission his altar.

I approached the task cautiously, and as I boxed up statues and other implements from the altar, I had a conversation with the guy from Galilee. I thanked him for what he had given me and done for me in the past, and then I explained why we were breaking up. I was honest about why it was time to let go, and thanked him for the time we had spent together. I think honesty is the best way to approach such situations.

Some deities are a part of our family for life, and others for only a few years or months. We learn what we need to from them, and then one of us moves on. There's no shame in that. It's simply how relationships work.

LTZ: I feel that all of the deities and spirits I work with are part of my family. I see some of my family members regularly, and others I keep in touch with very loosely. I still acknowledge the presence of such deities, but it may not be on the active main altar. I think the best way to avoid an awkward breakup is not to make commitments to deities that you don't feel strongly connected to in the first place. Practice clear communication and be direct. You don't *have* to have a certain set or number of deities, so don't add gods just because you feel pressured to have some sort of matched set or meet someone else's expectation.

Many thanks to all of our family, friends, and fans who submitted questions to us!

This book has been quite the adventure, born of late nights bonding over scotch, wine, and hard cider. We hope you, dear reader, have enjoyed your time sharing this adventure with us. Blessed altar building!

RESOURCES

The best place to buy altar supplies is your neighborhood Witch or metaphysical shop. Yes, it's super-easy to order things on Amazon these days, but local stores are important gathering places for our communities, and to keep them alive and vibrant we need to shop in them!

Statues

Dryad Design—http://dryaddesign.com

Maxine Miller—https://www.maxinemillerstudios.com

Mythic Images—http://theguidingtree.com

Pacific Trading—http://www.pacifictradingonline.com

Sacred Source—https://www.sacredsource.com

Other Altar Wares

AzureGreen—http://www.azuregreen.net

Gaean Allusions Pottery—http://www.gaeanallusions.com

Mists and clearing sprays—https://moonwaterelixirs.com

Nikol King (altar cloths and more)—
   https://www.nikolking.com

Owlkeyme Arts (icons, shrine and altar images, altar
   cloths)—http://www.owlkeyme.com

Rare Earth Designs (travel altars, icons, reliquary and
   apothecary cases)—http://www.rareearthdesigns.net and
   https://www.etsy.com/shop/RareEarthWoodworks

BIBLIOGRAPHY

Agrippa, Henry Cornelius. *Three Books of Occult Philosophy.* Edited and annotated by Donald Tyson. St. Paul, MN: Llewellyn Publications, 1992. First published 1533. Agrippa's works (and pseudo-works) can generally be found online, but this edition offers extensive notes and a lot of historical background. Totally worth the investment.

Burkert, Walter. *Greek Religion.* Translated by John Raffan. Cambridge, MA: Harvard University Press, 1985. Originally published in German in 1977. For over thirty years Burkert's book has been the go-to for anyone interested in ancient Greek religion.

Campanelli, Dan and Pauline. *Circles, Groves & Sanctuaries: Sacred Spaces of Today's Pagans.* St. Paul, MN: Llewellyn, 1992. Tempest and I are both huge fans of the Campanellis (something we found out while writing this book), and *Circles, Groves & Sanctuaries* was one of the few books on altars ever published until this volume. Sadly, Pauline passed away in 2001 and Dan in 2017. This particular volume is out of print, but can easily be found online at a reasonable price. All of the Campanellis' books are terrific.

Cicero, Chic, and Sandra Tabatha Cicero. *The Essential Golden Dawn: An Introduction to High Magic.* St. Paul, MN: Llewellyn, 2003. A highly readable look at the Golden Dawn tradition that makes it accessible to almost anyone.

Cunningham, Scott. *Wicca: A Guide for the Solitary Practitioner.* St. Paul, MN: Llewellyn, 1989. Cunningham's book is revolutionary for using the term *Wicca* in its title and for being the most complete and accessible 101 book when it was first released.

Curtis, Gregory. *The Cave Painters.* New York: Knopf, 2006. A little bit dated now, but still an extremely readable book on (very) early human art and religion.

Davies, Owen. *Grimoires: A History of Magic Books.* New York: Oxford University Press, 2009. A scholarly yet readable history of grimoires and other magickal texts.

Farrar, Janet and Stewart. *A Witches' Bible: The Complete Witches' Handbook.* Custer, WA: Phoenix Publishing, 1996. The two volumes that make up this one book were originally published as *The Witches' Way* (1984) and *Eight Sabbats for Witches* (1981). This one volume still remains the best introduction to Witchcraft in the tradition of Gerald Gardner and other early British Witches.

Gardner, Gerald. *Witchcraft Today* and *The Meaning of Witchcraft.* Published in 1954 and 1959, respectively. Gardner was the first modern public Witch, and while his books don't hold up all that well today, they have still been tremendously influential.

González-Wippler, Migene. *The Complete Book of Amulets & Talismans.* St. Paul, MN: Llewellyn, 1991. One of my (Jason's) first magickal books and still treasured, not to mention useful.

Hayden, Brian. *Shamans, Sorcerers, and Saints: A Prehistory of Religion.* Washington, DC: Smithsonian Books, 2003. A solid though somewhat speculative look at early religious practices, including those that predated modern humans.

Lady Sheba. *The Grimoire of Lady Sheba.* Originally published in 1972 by Llewellyn, my version is the reprint from 2001.

Larrington, Carolyne, trans. *The Poetic Edda.* Oxford: Oxford University Press, 1996. The Eddas are like *Bulfinch's Mythology*: every good Pagan should have a copy.

Murray, Margaret Alice. *The Witch-Cult in Western Europe.* This book was originally published in 1921 and is now available in a variety of editions. Murray's work helped spark the Witchcraft revival of the 1950s that has continued into the present day.

Nelson, John K. *A Year in the Life of a Shinto Shrine.* Seattle, WA: University of Washington Press, 1996. This book provides fascinating insight into Japanese shrine rituals and festivals.

Simek, Rudolf. *Dictionary of Northern Mythology.* Translated by Angela Hall. Rochester, NY: D. S. Brewer, 1993.

Valiente, Doreen. *Witchcraft For Tomorrow* and *The Charge of the Goddess. Tomorrow* was published in 1978 by Robert Hale, with *The Charge of the Goddess* coming out in 2014, fifteen years after her death. Although Tempest and I don't quote Doreen in this book, we are both huge fans of her work and it has informed our respective Witchcrafts tremendously. *Charge* is a collection of Doreen's poetry, and I think we've both read it in front of our various altars by candlelight.

To Write to the Authors

If you wish to contact the authors or would like more information about this book, please write to the authors in care of Llewellyn Worldwide and we will forward your request. Both the authors and the publisher appreciate hearing from you and learning of your enjoyment of this book and how it has helped you. Llewellyn Worldwide cannot guarantee that every letter written to the authors can be answered, but all will be forwarded. Please write to:

Laura Tempest Zakroff and Jason Mankey
Llewellyn Worldwide
2143 Wooddale Drive
Woodbury, MN 55125-2989

Please enclose a self-addressed stamped envelope for reply
or $1.00 to cover costs. If outside the USA, enclose
an international postal reply coupon.

Many of Llewellyn's authors have websites with additional information and resources. For more information, please visit our website:

WWW.LLEWELLYN.COM